A PORTRAIT OF
MILITARY AVIATION IN SOUTH AFRICA

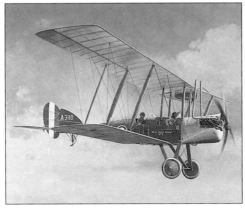 

R BELLIN ©

A portrait of
MILITARY AVIATION
IN SOUTH AFRICA

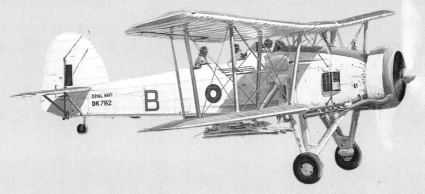

Ron Belling

OFFICIAL WAR ARTIST TO THE SOUTH AFRICAN AIR FORCE

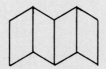

Midland Counties Publications

To Peg, Catherine and Robert

Acknowledgements

My grateful thanks and appreciation go to the following people who have assisted me in making this book possible.

Tony Badger
The late J. Barnes
Capt Dave Becker
Norma Besener
Bob Binnell
Cmdt Buck Buchanan
Capt Nick Carter
The late Nobby Clark
Col Gert de Beer
Cmdt J. van R. du Preez
Col George Duxbury
Maj Des Eden
H. A. Filley
Fleet Air Arm Museum
Roy Glover
Geoff Hamp-Adams
Clayton Holliday
The late Brian Hook
Dr Dennis Hoskin
Robert Johnston

Mike King
Percy Lindsay-Rae
Charles Louw
Dr Douglas McCallum
John McGillivray
Col Peter McGregor
The late Pat (Syd) Neave
Peter Oosthuisen
Leith Paxton
Ian Peddle
Cmdt Rod Penall
Mike Philips
Herman Potgieter
Donald Prentice
Royal Air Force Museum
Cmdt Graham Rochat
Donald Rodger (Port Elizabeth City Librarian)
Lt-Gen Bob Rogers
South African Air Force Museum
Cmdt Eric Schmullian

Capt Owen Smedley-Williams
Col Attie Smit
Cmdt Koos Smit
Cmdt Tony Smit
Ken Smy
Ivan Spring
Capt (SAN) R. D. Stephen
Ken Stewart
Keith Sutton
The late J. W. Taylor
Mel Templer
Brig 'Thack' Thackwray
The late Bill Todd
Bob Tunley
John Watts
Jack White
The late Warren Whitehead
Frank Wilson
Bert Yates (who also spent many hours during the war recording activities at the Port Elizabeth Airfield)

Louis Vosloo was the first person to view the completed set of paintings, and I acknowledge with gratitude his guidance regarding the publishing of the work, as well as his valuable constructive criticism.

Published by
Midland Counties Publications
24 The Hollow
Earl Shilton
LEICESTER LE9 7NA, UK
Tel 0455 47256

Text and illustrations © R. R. Belling 1989

First published 1989

House editor Jan Schaafsma
Designer Etienne van Duyker
Cover designer Willem Jordaan

Typesetting by Diatype Setting
Reproduction by Hirt & Carter
Printed and bound in Singapore

ISBN 0 904597 59 8

Contents

R BELLIN
© 82

Introduction

In recent years there has been a growing interest in the history of aviation, and many books have been published on the subject, with detailed research on virtually every aspect of aeronautics. These books have illustrated the phenomenal rate at which aviation has evolved, and the way in which it has become, in the process, a manifestation of man's ability to meet political and commercial demands, while at the same time profoundly changing the interaction between nations. And for the artist, a dynamic new world was created.

World War II, with its awe-inspiring developments in the field of aviation, has become the main area of research for many air historians. Of relevance to the present work is the observation of many of these historians that we have taken for granted the many thousands of machines in operation during those stormy years, only to realise, too late, that many types no longer exist. Fortunately the restoration of wrecks and the preservation of historical aircraft by institutions and individuals ranging from large museums to private owners has increased in scope, but unfortunately many such projects lose their historical value – despite high structural integrity – because of inaccurate finishing.

It is also clear that no fully illustrated history of military aviation in South Africa has ever been produced. My aim in publishing this work is therefore to portray the unique and fascinating visual richness of the many machines of the SAAF and other air arms that have operated from this country. This work is not intended as a definitive statement, but, hopefully, as the beginning of a new chapter on a neglected field of South African history. It is not a concise record of operations nor a detailed technical description of aircraft, as these aspects are already adequately covered in other books. Rather the paintings are a personal reflection of my experiences from 1938, since when, as an incurable enthusiast, I have sketched, modelled and photographed aeroplanes, accumulating in the process a great deal of material which was to become a valuable source of information for this project. It must be stressed, however, that the first 15 paintings, covering the period 1917-1937 (the years before my time) are contemplative portrayals based on extensive research and discussions with flying veterans.

Port Elizabeth is the background for most of the paintings simply because I was privileged to live near the airfield (built close to the city centre and busy port) and was therefore able to record most of the aircraft using the base during the war years. Despite the apparent narrowness of the locale, it will be clear from the remarkably broad scope of the subject matter that this is no drawback, as very few aircraft operating in South Africa did not make an appearance at Port Elizabeth. In addition the development of the airfield, as portrayed in this book, was in general paralleled by others throughout the country.

A brief comment is in order on the conceptual structure of the paintings themselves. In recreating the famous aircraft, authentic incidents of historical significance have been portrayed, without the histrionics of combat. Operational flying at the coast was mainly for the protection of shipping from the constant danger of the ever-present U-boats, which made it imperative that ships and the dynamic relationship of sea and sky should play a significant part in many of the compositions. It was with a tinge of nostalgia, however, that these scenes were painted, as most of the ships portrayed have long since gone to the breakers' yards.

Many of the works will, I hope, intrigue and surprise informed readers. For example, postwar Lockheed PV-1 Venturas are usually represented by artists with pale grey undersides, but actually they were nearly all finished with a pale yellow-grey-green officially referred to as 'Sky'. Others wore a variation of Sky with a brown cast, while some had a darker green tone. As another example, the portrayal (possibly the first) of one of the rare predominantly white Lockheed B-34 Venturas operated by 25 Squadron during 1942-1943 was painted from documentation kept in my files for 25 years until I had confirmation of the example's code letter.

In anticipation of the inevitable question why only a few current SAAF aircraft are represented in camouflage schemes, my answer is that space precluded a repetition of the present types so well recorded and photographed by experts such as Dave Becker, Herman Potgieter and Louis Vosloo. Most of our present aircraft are therefore shown in their original metal finishes.

It is my sincere wish that the reader should gain some insight into the colourful world of South African aviation and experience some of the pleasure and nostalgia which I enjoyed while working on this project.

Ron Belling
Port Elizabeth
November 1988

After completing the first long-distance flight in South Africa in 1917,
Maj Allister Miller comes in to land at the Port Elizabeth
Golf Club course in his Royal Aircraft Factory BE 2E.

Royal Aircraft Factory BE 2E

At 11h30 on 7 November 1917 thousands of excited Port Elizabethans, waiting at the Port Elizabeth Golf Club, sighted a speck in the western sky – the first aeroplane to visit the city. After making a long right-hand turn over the business area, the BE 2E, trailing puffs of smoke from twin vertical exhaust pipes, lined up for an approach to the golf course.

Approaching at what seemed like a great speed, the machine touched down on the 18th fairway, and the excited crowd surged forward from both sides. Unable to avoid a white-marked bunker, the aeroplane ended up on its nose, with a splintered propeller and damaged undercarriage. Fortunately the pilot, Maj Allister Miller, and observer, Sgt Way, were uninjured. It had taken them less than six hours at an average speed of 70 mph (113 km/h) to complete the first long-distance flight in the Union of South Africa, and in so doing they established military flying in the country.

Starting at Youngsfield in Cape Town, with Port Elizabeth as its first destination, the flight had been planned as a recruiting tour of the country. With the co-operation of the Union Government, the Royal Flying Corps Mission established at Youngsfield in October 1917 included Maj Miller, Lt Bagshaw, Sgt Way and Cpl Streeter. Two new BE 2E biplanes were donated by the British community in Rio de Janeiro and named 'Rio de Janeiro Britons' Nos 1 and 2. On the evening of 23 October 1917 Maj Miller tested 'No 2' (A-3110), flying up to 4 000 ft (1 219 m) over False Bay at speeds of up to 80 mph (128 km/h) without a hitch.

After the damage to 'No 2' was repaired at Port Elizabeth, the tour continued, and by 29 December 1917 Maj Miller had accepted 700 candidates for training in the RFC. In April 1918, while flying from Dundee to Pietermaritzburg, 'No 2' suffered another mishap when it lost a wheel, but Maj Miller managed to land the machine without damage. The missing wheel was later found on a farm and returned by courtesy of the South African Railways. On 19 October 1919 Lt Gearing delivered 'No 2' to the Union Defence authorities at Roberts Heights as the first of 100 military aeroplanes comprising the Imperial Gift from Britain – the beginning of the SAAF.

With a maze of rigging and a long-span upper mainplane of 40 ft 9 in (12,42 m), the BE

Major Allister Miller.

2E came in for unfounded, abusive criticism by aircrews who rumoured that the upper wing collapsed during aerobatics or developed an uncontrollable flutter at high speeds. Nevertheless the type carried out an enormous amount of spotting for the artillery, and by 1918 nearly 3 000 were in service.

Built by the Royal Aircraft Factory, the BE 2E was a two-seater reconnaissance biplane which first appeared on operations over the Battle of the Somme in 1916. Powered by a 90 hp (67 kW) RAF 1A air-cooled engine (a V8 Renault with larger cylinders), the BE 2E attained a maximum speed of 82 mph (132 km/h), a climb rate of 182 ft/min (55 m/min) and a service ceiling of 11 000 ft (3 353 m).

Notes on the finish

The upper surface finish of 'No 2', like most aircraft built for overseas RFC service, was Pigmented/Protective Cellulose (Specification No 10 or 12). Clear varnish was applied to the undersides, which, when viewed from below, seemed semi-transparent and, as usual, had a patchy appearance. Medium Grey pigmented oil varnish was applied to all metal panels, with clear varnish on timber struts. All lettering was White, and the insignia Vermillion, White and Ultramarine. The incomplete underside roundels comprised the Vermillion circle.

Birth of the SAAF

On 20 August 1920 the SAAF was officially formed. Sir Pierre van Ryneveld, the Director of Air Services, was to lay the foundation of the new structure with a small nucleus of officers and men of the Permanent Force who had gained Air Force experience during World War I.

The inception of the SAAF was entirely due to the splendid Imperial Gift to South Africa by the British Government, which comprised 100 Avro 504s, DH 9s, SE5 As, a few DH 4s and one BE 2E, complete with engines and 28 spare engines, 250 transport vehicles (including workshop lorries, three-ton lorries, cars and motorcycles), steel framework for 20 permanent hangars, and 30 wood-and-canvas Bessoneau hangars, complete wireless equipment for fitting two squadrons of 18 aircraft each, complete photographic material for two squadrons, 50 000 gallons (225 000 ℓ) of special aircraft engine oil, 20 000 gallons (90 000 ℓ) of paints, varnishes and dope, and tools and workshop equipment to maintain all the aircraft for a year.

The plan was to have one squadron of 18 machines fully operational during 1920-1921, to be followed by a second unit a year later. Co-operation between the SAAF and the RAF, and the influence of British aviation on South Africa, was to endure for many years – in fact until the annual 'Operation Capex' exercises were discontinued well after World War II.

The Solomon brothers' two de Havilland 6s flying over Port Elizabeth in 1920. The North and South Jettys are clearly visible on either side of the Baakens River mouth, while the Walmer Castle, *recently returned from war service, lies at anchor in Algoa Bay.*

De Havilland 6

Frank Solomon and his brother Shirley, Cape Town aviators recently returned from the war, purchased two de Havilland 6 aircraft at a Ministry of Munitions sale of surplus aircraft in Britain in August 1919. Among the many machines no longer required by the RAF after the cessation of hostilities, Nos C-9448 and C-9449 were shipped to South Africa as G-EAMK and G-EAML, and during November the Solomons started flying operations from Muizenberg and Green Point.

On what was possibly the first undertaking of its kind in the Union, both machines were chartered for a business trip to Port Elizabeth, where they arrived on 24 January 1920, landing at the 'New' Fairview Aerodrome, which was to serve the city for more than a decade. During the following week their angular 'cut-off' appearance became a familiar sight over Algoa Bay as joyrides were offered at a cost of three guineas for ten minutes.

On Boxing Day 1920 one of the aircraft, flown by Capt Hemming and with three passengers aboard, flew into a 60-ft (18 m) high chimney near Green Point Common and all aboard were killed when the machine burst

into flames. In April 1922 the successful flying career of the remaining machine also came to an end when it experienced an engine failure during a test flight from Muizenberg with Shirley Solomon at the controls. With insufficient height to land on the beach, the DH 6 struck a sand dune, overturned, and was wrecked. Fortunately the pilot and both passengers were uninjured. The story has an interesting sequel in that aviation historian Louis Vosloo discovered the remains of this machine in an upholsterer's workshop in Muizenberg in 1977.

Designed by Capt Geoffry de Havilland in 1916, the DH 6, a product of the Aircraft Manufacturing Company (Airco), had been specifically conceived as a primary trainer for the Royal Flying Corps. For ease of production the wire-braced timber airframe with its fabric covering was entirely square-cut or angled – the only visible curves being the wing camber, cockpit cutout and wheels.

Like the BE 2E, the DH 6's engine was a 90 hp (67 kW) RAF 1A, which developed an underpowered performance so exceptionally docile that instability had to be incorporated into its flying characteristics for the benefit of pupils. A stately top speed of 66 mph (106 km/h) earned it the dubious nickname of 'The Clutching Hand' or 'Sky Hook'.

When the Avro 504 was adopted as the standard RFC trainer, the DH 6 was slowly phased out. However, due to increased U-boat activity, the type made a come-back in an anti-submarine role, and nearly 200 examples flew along the British coastline during the last year of the war.

Notes on the finish
It is evident from the brown cast of the finish on the DH 6 remains now at the SAAF Museum that Pigmented/Protective Cellulose 12 was probably applied according to the British overseas specification. If by chance the aircraft had been repainted in the Union, RFC/RAF PC 12 dope as supplied to the SAAF would have been used. Instead of the British registration, both machines had the word 'Shell' painted in bold yellow letters on their fuselage sides when they were flown to Port Elizabeth.

Vought UO-1

In 1920 the US Navy embarked on a new light cruiser building programme. Referred to as scout cruisers, the seventh and eighth (USS *Concorde* and USS *Trenton*, completed in November 1923 and April 1924 respectively), undertook shakedown cruises to South Africa. Arriving in Algoa Bay in February 1924, *Concorde*, sporting four funnels, made an interesting comparison with HMS *Birmingham*, flagship of the Africa Station. Aboard *Concorde* was the first shipboard marine aircraft to be seen along the South African coast – a Vought UO-1 observation floatplane. When USS *Trenton* called at South African ports in June 1924, her UO-1, referred to as a hydroplane, performed daring exhibitions of 'stunt' flying by a young American flyer, Lt Hilton.

The evolution of the UO-1 began in 1918 when the newly-formed Lewis & Vought Company produced the VE-7 and VE-9 fighters. Designed by Chance M. Vought, they were adapted from the de Havilland 4, with wings, tailplane and undercarriage almost identical to the British machine. After World War I the newly-named Chance Vought Corporation modified the VE-7 shape by streamlining the fuselage with stringered formers, and fitting redesigned vertical tail surfaces. A 220 hp (165 kW) Wright J-5 engine replaced the 180 hp (135 kW) 3 Hispano-Wright on the new FU-1 fighter, as it then became known.

The next major development was to convert the FU-1 into a catapult-launched, shipboard observation seaplane. Designated UO-1, the basic airframe had been retained, but it was fitted with a 200 hp (150 kW) Wright J-3 engine housed in an attractive rounded nose with a large spinner, a second cockpit for the observer was positioned ahead of the pilot's station, and floats replaced the wheeled undercarriage. With a large, smooth, timber-covered central float, wingtip stabilising pontoons, well-shaped fuselage and fighter-like performance, the UO-1 was a trendsetter. It had a speed of 124 mph (200 km/h), a climb rate of 1 000 ft/min (302 m/min) and a ceiling of 18 800 ft (5 486 m).

Notes on the finish

All fabric surfaces were finished with Aluminium enamel and all metal panels with Light Gray, while spar varnish was adopted for all struts. The timber-covered float and metal pontoons were in protective Light Gray. According to an August 1919 directive the insignia were Red, White and Insignia Blue. The latter, which replaced the World War I Ultramarine, is a deep indigo still in use by the US Air Force and US Navy. The star insignia on the wings had a diameter equal to the distance from aileron leading edge to wing leading edge, and in this case was positioned further inboard to accommodate the positions of the pontoons. Rudder stripes were applied, and the aircraft number, believed to be A-6614, appeared in small Black numerals on the White stripe.

With USS Trenton *in the background, Lt Hilton puts the scout cruiser's Vought UO-1 hydroplane through its paces over Table Bay.*

De Havilland 9

Starting in early 1925 for a trial period of 3½ months, a coastal mail service from Durban to Cape Town via East London, Port Elizabeth and Mossel Bay was planned by the SAAF, with Lt-Col Sir Pierre van Ryneveld, Director of Air Services, in charge. By the end of January the necessary facilities were installed at the various relay bases. At Port Elizabeth, for example, two Bessoneau hangars transported by rail were erected on a site cleared at the Fairview Aerodrome.

On 23 February 1925 Maj Holthouse, accompanied by Sgt McQueen, arrived from Durban on a tour of inspection. Their aeroplane, a de Havilland 9 (No 141), was one of the first to receive the new post-war Silver finish. On the following day five DH 9s arrived over Port Elizabeth. Circling over the city, the machines (in wartime drab finish) impressed the public, being the first SAAF aircraft to operate from the Eastern Cape.

Generally this major operation went ahead without problems. Because of dense mist at the coast, however, Mossel Bay had to be abandoned as a base in favour of Oudtshoorn. In another incident one of the machines based at Port Elizabeth (No 128, flown by Lt Burger) was blown over onto its back by a gust of wind, but was fortunately not badly damaged and within a week was flying again. The trial period ended on 27 June 1925 when six machines, led by Lt-Gen Kenneth van der Spuy, flew out of Port Elizabeth. Considered a great success, the service afforded the SAAF

Piloting one of the de Havilland 9s which inaugurated an experimental coastal mail service, Lt Burger circles the Port Elizabeth central area on 24 February 1925.

valuable experience in coastal flying, map reading and logistics.

The DH 9 was originally built as a replacement for the DH 4 light day bomber, but did not live up to initial expectations. The Armstrong Siddeley Puma engine was expected to deliver 300 hp (225 kW), but had to be derated to 230 hp (172 kW), leaving the machine underpowered and with a performance no better than its predecessor. Because of a massive production program – 2 166 were built – the DH 9 was, however, committed to service. Although at times not able to maintain altitude with a full bomb load of 460 lb (209 kg), DH 9s nevertheless carried out strategic bombing raids over German border towns on a large scale before the Armistice.

The type's flying surfaces were identical to those of the DH 4, but changes to its fuselage included modifications to accommodate the Puma engine, and moving the pilot's cockpit further aft so as to afford a better all-round view. With a timber frame and fabric covering (apart from the forward fuselage, which was built of plywood sheeting) the DH 9 was a well-proportioned machine with the typical aesthetically pleasing de Havilland vertical tail surfaces.

Notes on the finish

The top surface finish for South Africa's DH 9s was Protective/Pigmented Cellulose 12 (or very brown PC 10), in accordance with RFC and, later, RAF specifications for aircraft operating overseas. The undersides of the flying surfaces were finished in clear varnish.

The SAAF insignia was an adaption of the RAF roundel. The existing Vermillion and Ultramarine were retained, but Green and 'Gold' replaced the White, with 'Gold' adjoining the Ultramarine. All four colours were of equal proportions and the thin White surround was retained. The SAAF serial number on the rear fuselage in White had a narrow matching band. Silver was introduced as a more practical aircraft finish for the SAAF during 1925. One of the first aircraft to wear the new paintwork was a DH 9 (No 141). The four-colour insignia were retained, with the serial number in Black and struts finished with PC 12 or Brown.

With Maj Holthouse (Inspector of Installations) at the controls, a de Havilland 9 flies over HMS Repulse near Plettenberg Bay. The battle-cruiser carried out a coastal cruise while HRH The Prince of Wales, who sailed in her to South Africa, was undertaking a tour of the hinterland.

Some Aircraft Developments in Germany

During the two world wars, South Africa's Imperial commitments led to her fighting on the side of Britain, and therefore the fertile German aviation industry was on the enemy side. However, developments in Germany played a large part in world aviation, and therefore influenced aviation in South Africa as well.

While the SAAF was being created, the Armistice Agreement specified that Germany's Luftwaffe was to be totally dismantled, and among the many fine aircraft that were destroyed, two stand out as exceptional.

While not the fastest fighter of the time, the Fokker DVII was remarkable for its ability to outmanoeuvre most opponents. Its thick-sectioned, unbraced cantilever wing had remarkable stalling characteristics which allowed it to hang on the propeller and fire into a victim's belly. Initially powered by the 160 hp (120 kW) Mercedes IIIB engine, its performance was further improved when the new 185 hp (138 kW) BMW III, the first production engine of the then new company, was installed. Decendants of the DVII were the Fokker Super Universal and the Avro Anson, and both were to play an important role in South African aviation.

The Junkers J 9 was the world's first all-metal monoplane fighter. It was also powered by the BMW III engine, and introduced a form of construction – a corrugated Duralumin skin – which was to play a major role in post-war civil flying.

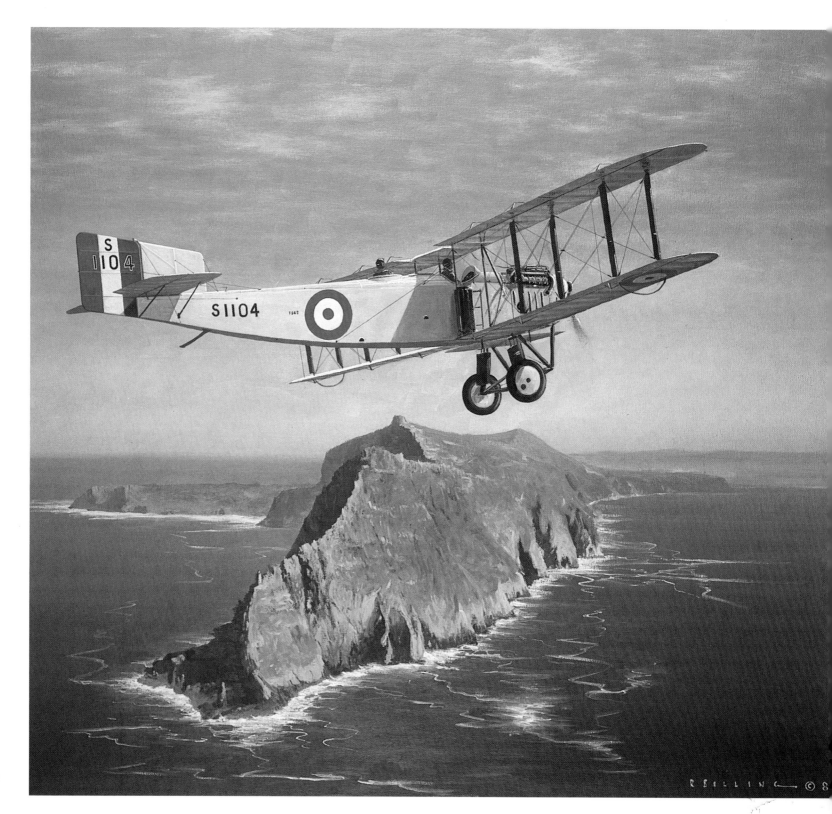

One of the first four RAF *aircraft to visit South Africa, a Fairey IIID gracefully banks over the dramatic background of the Cape of Good Hope.*

Fairey IIID

At 10h00 on 2 April 1926 four RAF Fairey IIID biplanes made their appearance over Pretoria, an event which marked the beginning of many years of co-operation between the SAAF and the RAF. Greeted by a large crowd, the Silver aeroplanes gracefully landed at Zwartkop, where 45 SAAF machines were lined up to honour their distinguished visitors. These, the first RAF aircraft to fly to the Union, had also successfully undertaken the RAF's first long-range formation flight. Referred to as the Cape Flight (as Cape Town was their final destination), the unit was formed at Northolt in late 1925. The aircraft departed from Heliopolis on 1 March 1926 and landed at Cape Town on 12 April. When they touched down, the spare propeller on one of the machines – slung above the undercarriage – was seen to be covered in oil.

On their return flight to Britain the aircraft were converted from wheeled to floatplane undercarriages at Aboukir and arrived at Lee-on-Solent on 21 June 1926. Apart from the oil leak on one of the aircraft, the flight of 14 000 miles (22 500 km) was achieved without any mechanical failures.

With attractive high aspect-ratio wings the Fairy IIID's incongruous square-sectioned fuselage, tail assembly and clumsy undercarriage betrayed its World War I ancestry. A development of the 1918 Fairey IIIC, the Fairey IIID was a three-seater general-purpose biplane which could be used for bombing, spotting or reconnaissance, fitted either with wheels or with twin floats as a seaplane. Powered by a 450 hp (336 kW) Napier Lion triple-bank 12-cylinder engine and with a top speed of 120 mph (193 km/h), the type had a maximum range of 550 miles (885 km).

Notes on the finish

The overall finish was Silver, with all the struts finished in Brown. Red, White and Blue insignia and rudder stripes were worn. World War I insignia colours may have been used on some machines.

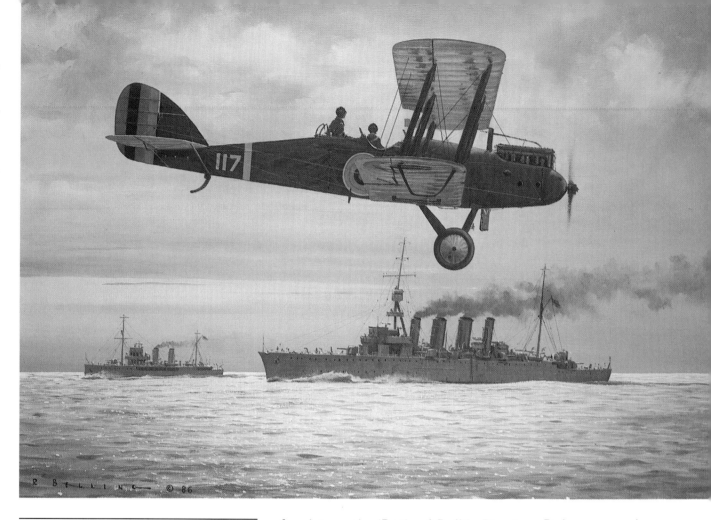

De Havilland 9

On 19 June 1926 four de Havilland 9s arrived in Port Elizabeth to take part in naval manoeuvres – the first such manoeuvres in South Africa to include the Air Force. The cruiser HMS *Lowestoft* and her escort sloop HMS *Verbena* lay in Algoa Bay while the Africa Station flagship, HMS *Birmingham*, and her sloop, HMS *Wallflower*, were anchored off Bird Island. The latter were expected to attack the units at Port Elizabeth, while the role of the SAAF was to monitor shipping movements and to attack warships at night as they neared the coast, using flower bombs to mark any strikes. However, *Birmingham* and *Wallflower* left Bird Island unexpectedly and instead of appearing off Port Elizabeth as planned, made a dash for East London in a surprise attack referred to as the 'Battle of Buffalo River'. Their initiative was lost, however, for one of the DH 9s based at Woodbrook Aerodrome near East London spotted the ships while still at sea. Although coming off second best to the SAAF in this instance, *Birmingham* had a good operational war record. Built in 1914, she saw continual action in World War I, and had the honour of being the first to sink a U-boat (U-15), by ramming her on 1 August 1914.

The 48 DH 9s supplied to the Union as part of the Imperial Gift performed very well with the SAAF. Apart from the experimental mail service (see p 12) and naval manoeuvres mentioned above, they were regularly involved in exercises with RAF units on their annual visits to the Union. One of the Imperial Gift DH 9s still exists, but unfortunately this valuable SAAF aeroplane is badly finished and poorly displayed in the South African National Museum of Military History.

During manoeuvres in June 1926 the cruiser HMS Birmingham *and the sloop HMS* Wallflower *made an unexpected dash for East London, but were intercepted by a de Havilland 9. The observer, attached to the aircraft by a monkey chain, is standing in his cockpit.*

Dornier Merkur

On the morning of 21 February 1927 a high-wing monoplane seaplane winged its way across Algoa Bay, gracefully flew over the Swartkops River shoreline, crossed over the centre of town, and then flew out to sea in the direction of Cape Town. The Swissair Dornier Merkur, flown by Lt Walter Mittelholzer, had taken off from the Buffalo River at East London about 70 minutes earlier on the last leg of a flight from Zurich, down Africa, to Cape Town. His passengers – scientists who were making a study of the river estuaries covered by the flight – had intended to land on the Swartkops River, but were advised not to do so by the Port Captain, who was concerned about excessive debris floating on the waterway. They therefore landed in Table Bay after a six-hour flight from East London. After the flight, which was accomplished without a hitch, the Merkur was shipped back to Europe aboard the new Deutsche Ost-Afrika Linie liner *Toledo*.

Built by Dornier, the Merkur was of an all-metal construction and carried six passengers and a crew of two. Thirty-five of these machines successfully served on Lufthansa night routes which had then recently been inaugurated. The Merkur's powerplant was one of the most powerful engines of the time, the BMW VI V-12, which developed 600 hp (450 kW). Evolved from the BMW IIIA via the IV and V by a design team headed by Helmut Sachse, the BMW VI was adopted by the Soviet Union as their standard V-12 engine, with the designation M-17.

Notes on the finish
The Merkur's overall finish was Silver, with broad Red chordwise wingbands which bore the registration letters. The letters CH were painted in White on the overall Red rudder, while the Black trim included the number 171 on the fuselage sides.

Opposite: *While on a scientific flight to Cape Town, this Swissair Dornier Merkur, flown by Lt Walter Mittelholzer, skims over the Swartkops River mouth.*

Below: *The Merkur in Table Bay.*

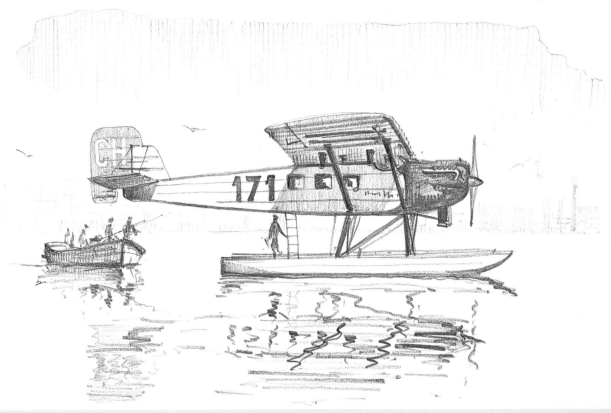

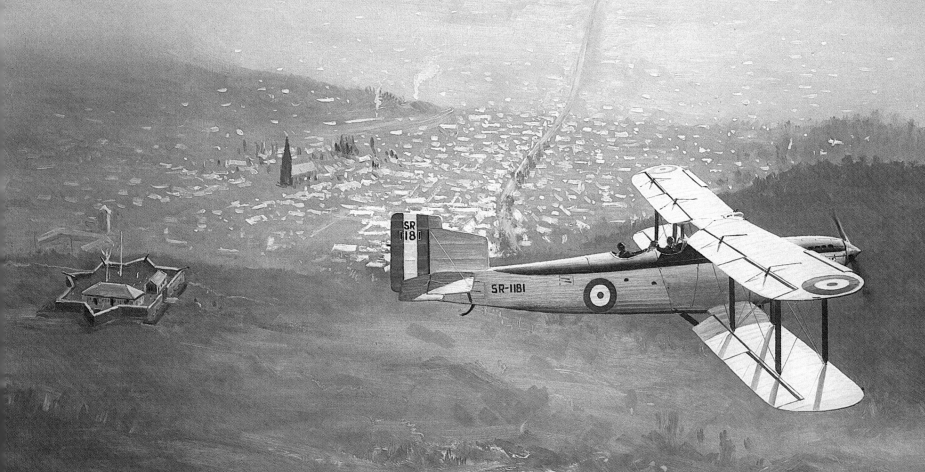

Fairey IIIF

Due to the successful Cape Flight of 1926, the RAF decided to undertake similar flights as an annual event. In 1927, therefore, 47 Squadron flew their new Fairey IIIFs, recently 'off the secret list' to the Union. After visiting Cape Town, the four machines flew along the coast to Port Elizabeth, from where they continued to Grahamstown. Manoeuvres were carried out with the Prince Alfred's Guards, First City Regiment and Kaffrarian Rifles, as well as with five SAAF de Havilland 9s. In 1928 and 1929 47 Squadron returned to the Union, while in 1930 the flight was undertaken by 14 Squadron, also with Fairey IIIFs.

In 1929, when 47 Squadron arrived in Port Elizabeth en route to Grahamstown, their four Fairey IIIFs sported the earlier, angular fins. Built originally for the Royal Navy, these aircraft were later withdrawn and reconstructed as two-seaters for the RAF (the Fleet Air Arm aircraft were three-seaters). Rebuilt aircraft were identified by the inclusion of the letter R in the serial number. On their return flight to Egypt, SR1181 crashed at Bulawayo, with the loss of both crew members.

Although the wing of the Fairey IIIF was the same as that fitted to the IIID, the similarity ended there. With a beautifully contoured nose, well-proportioned tail and cleaned-up undercarriage, the IIIF proved a very successful day bomber and general-purpose type, serving at home and overseas as a land or floatplane with the RAF and FAA. The new XIA version of the Napier Lion engine, developing 570 hp (425 kW), was fitted to the IIIF, considerably improving its performance as compared to that of the IIID.

Notes on the finish
In addition to their standard overall Silver finish, 47 Squadron aircraft wore the matt Black fuselage decking applied to RAF aircraft operating overseas. All struts were Brown and standard. Red, White and Blue insignia and rudder stripes were worn.

CAMS 37²

When the new French cruiser *Duquesne* visited Algoa Bay in April 1929, she had on board two examples of the first operational naval flying boat to be seen in South Africa, apart from the attractive Short Singapore in which Sir Alan Cobham had flown across Africa a few months earlier. Like her slightly modified sisters *Suffren*, *Foch*, *Colbert* and *Dupleix*, *Duquesne* was of the Tourville class, and these ships each carried two CAMS 37² flying boats.

Built by Chantiers Aéro-Maritimes de la Seine – between the wars one of France's leading manufacturers of waterborne aircraft – the CAMS 37 was designed in 1924 and flown for the first time in 1926. It was the company's most successful aircraft, with excellent sea handling characteristics, sturdy construction and a good performance in the air. They were built in large numbers during a production run of seven years. Operating as a three-seater bombing or coastal reconnaissance flying boat, the 37² also proved to be an ideal shipboard observation machine, serving aboard French cruisers. Like the later Supermarine Walrus, which it closely resembled, one 37² version was amphibious.

The unstaggered timber-framed flying surfaces were fabric-covered, while the fuselage had ash and spruce formers with main timber rails to support the double-skinned lower hull, built of mahogany covered with plywood. The engine, a Lorraine 12 E6 12-cylinder W pusher which developed 450 hp (335 kW), was mounted on struts between the wings, with the radiator neatly fitted on the nacelle front.

At least eight 37²s were in service at the outbreak of World War II, and one was still serving in Indo-China in 1942.

Notes on the finish
The finish was the standard scheme for French maritime aircraft at the time. All top surfaces, including struts, were finished in Blue-Grey very near to FS 36118, but slightly more blue. The undersides finish was almost like FS 35189, but slightly less blue. The roundel Red was almost the same as BS 538, and the Blue near to FS 35190. Although the FS matt standards are referred to, the hull had a high-gloss finish, and the flying surfaces a semi-gloss finish.

Above: *The CAMS 37² carried by the French cruiser* Duquesne *flies low over its mother ship in Algoa Bay in 1929.*

Opposite: *With the early morning sun reflecting off their upper surfaces, four Fairey IIIFs of 47 Squadron (RAF) arrive over Grahamstown in 1929. Fort Selwyn is clearly visible in the left foreground.*

Fokker Super Universal

With the inauguration of an internal South African air mail service in August 1929, Maj Allister Miller had achieved his objective, planned since the end of World War 1. Union Airways, with its headquarters at Fairview Aerodrome in Port Elizabeth, began operations with a fleet of five de Havilland Gipsy Moths, some fitted with small cockpit canopies to protect passengers from the elements. Operating successfully under conditions which by present-day standards were appalling, Union Airways later took delivery of their first cabin monoplane, a de Havilland Puss Moth, and in addition ordered a new Fokker mailplane from the United States. Maj Miller purchased this aircraft through General Motors, who had recently established a motor assembly plant in Port Elizabeth.

Arriving in Port Elizabeth by sea and assembled at Fairview in just more than a week, the big six-passenger monoplane made its first flight on 22 January 1930. The 'Red and Yellow Monster' as it was called, made its first passenger-carrying flight from Port Elizabeth to Cape Town on 30 January, in a time of 3 hours 40 minutes. Although it was pre-dated in Europe by the trend-setting Junkers F 13, the Super Universal was the first 'airliner' to operate in the Union.

The Union Airways Fokker, powered by a 420 hp (315 kW) Pratt & Whitney Wasp engine, proved popular and was always in great demand with passengers. On 31 December it crashed at Kaysers Beach 28 miles west of East London in thick mist, with Maj Miller at the controls. The aircraft was a write-off, but due to the pilot's exceptional skill no-one was injured.

Notes on the finish

With the exception of the wing upper surfaces, which were Silver, all flying surfaces were Post Office Red. All natural metal surfaces were buffed, while the fuselage and vertical tail surfaces were deep Chrome Yellow. The trim and registration number were Black.

A Fokker Super Universal, piloted by Capt Bellin, flies dangerously low over rough seas off Cape St Francis, having just passed through a heavy squall in an attempt to deliver the mail in time for the departure of the Union-Castle mailship from Cape Town.

Forebear of the famous 'Annie'

The Fokker Super Universal had distinguished forebears, and in turn had a significant influence on the design of one of the most famous British aircraft – the Avro Anson. When World War I ended, the military operations of the Fokker organisation ceased in Germany. Prior to its re-establishment in Holland, the company's chief designer, Reinhold Platz (creator of the Fokker DVII – arguably the best fighter of World War I), developed a passenger-carrying high-wing monoplane. Between fifty and sixty examples of this type, known as the Fokker F-III, were built.

The next Fokker passenger aircraft, the F-VII designed by Walter Rethel, was fitted with an efficient thick-sectioned, plywood-covered, cantilever high wing. Incidentally, Rethel later became chief engineer of the Arado-Handelsgesellschaft before joining Bayerische Flugzeugwerke (Messerschmitt), where he worked on the designs of the Bf 109 and Bf 110 fighters.

In 1925, while residing in the United States, Anthony Fokker requested Platz, in Holland, to redesign the F-VII as a three-engined aircraft to compete in the US market. This request was carried out in a remarkably short time and by late 1925 the Fokker F-VIIA/3m arrived in the US, where it won the Ford Reliability Tour. In the US Fokker amalgamated with the Atlantic Aircraft Company, and as the Fokker Atlantic Aircraft Corporation built the Super Universal, a modified F-VII, for production in the US.

In Britain the F-VIIB/3m was built under licence, with the designation Avro 618 'Ten'. In 1933 Imperial Airways submitted a specification to Avro for a fast, long-range twin-engined charter aircraft with a retractable undercarriage. Designer Roy Chadwick modified the Fokker airframe by placing the one-piece wooden mainplane in the lower position and streamlining the fuselage by fitting formers and stringers with fabric covering – and the Avro 652 and famous 652A Anson had been born. Chadwick went on to design some of the most famous Avro aircraft, including the Tutor, Manchester, Lancaster, York, Shackleton, Vulcan and Tudor airliner. He was killed on 23 August 1947 when the Tudor 2 prototype in which he was flying crashed on take-off.

De Havilland 66 Hercules

During the morning of 26 May 1932 Port Elizabethans were surprised to see a large silver biplane circle the city, a powerful throbbing emanating from its three engines. The aircraft – an Imperial Airways de Havilland 66 Hercules named 'City of Delhi' – was en route from Cape Town to its first refuelling station at Beaufort West, but had strayed from its route, and was forced to land at Fairview to refuel.

Capable of transporting a crew of three and fourteen passengers (or seven passengers and cargo), the Hercules was a large machine. Except for the metal-framed fuselage, it conformed to the de Havilland company's standard of timber framing with fabric covering. Its three Bristol Jupiter engines, each of which developed 420 hp (315 kW), were designed by Roy Fedden, who later created the outstanding range of Bristol radial engines which culminated in the Centaurus. Built specifically for Imperial Airways, the Hercules entered South African service when the British airline inaugurated a London-to-Cape service in January 1932 after a great deal of frustration.

The first Hercules built (G-EBMW, 'City of Cairo') arrived in South Africa in October 1931 by sea. It had crashed in the East Indies and was off-loaded at the Durban docks in transit to Germiston, where Imperial Airways were planning to use it for spares at the new workshops they had established for the forthcoming service. Hercules G-EBMX ('City of Delhi'), built in 1926, was the second machine off the production line, which closed after the completion of eleven aircraft. In 1934-1935 G-AAJH ('City of Basra'), G-ABMT ('City of Cape Town'), and G-EBMX ('City of Delhi') were taken over by the SAAF as Nos 260, 261 and 262, serving until 1943.

Notes on the finish
The overall finish was Silver, with Black trim and struts.

A Fairey IIIF seaplane moored at the South Jetty, Port Elizabeth, with HMS Dorsetshire alongside the new Charl Malan quay. The Campanile in the background commemorates the 1820 British Settlers.

Fairey IIIF seaplane

After two years under construction, the first stage of the new Port Elizabeth harbour was officially opened on 20 October 1933. The recently completed cruiser HMS *Dorsetshire*, flagship of the Cape (Africa) Station, flying the flag of Vice-Adml Sir Edward Evans (of the Broke), was the first ship to dock at the completed section of the Charl Malan quay. Her spotter seaplane, a Fairey IIIF Mk IIIB, flew over the city, landed in the harbour, and moored alongside the South Jetty.

In 1941 *Dorsetshire* was back in South African waters after having taken part in the sinking of the German battleship *Bismarck* a few weeks earlier – but on Easter Sunday, 1942, she and her sister HMS *Cornwall* were sunk by Japanese bombers south of Ceylon.

The F version of the classic Fairey III design was a three-seater catapult seaplane for spotter-reconnaissance duties, and served on many Royal Navy capital ships and cruisers. By 1935 the type was retired when Hawker Ospreys entered service.

Notes on the finish
Royal Navy aircraft of the time, like their RAF counterparts, were Silver overall with matt Black fuselage decking and Brown struts. Standard insignia were worn.

Hawker Fury I

By 1933 the Port Elizabeth Municipality had recognised the necessity for a new airfield to replace the Fairview Aerodrome, and months of indecision ended when a site in South End was selected. Set about 5 km from the city centre immediately south of Victoria Park and the attractive suburb of Walmer, the 1 000 x 1 000 yd (914 x 914 m) field was built on comparatively level ground. Port Jackson willow, imported during the previous century from Australia to consolidate the driftsand, covered the limestone and seasand that stretched to the Indian Ocean 8 km further south. A single hangar, ancillary buildings and concrete apron comprised the new aerodome, officially opened on 23 May 1936 with an air pageant, followed by additional shows on the next two days.

The show was opened by a sight never before seen in the city: 40 aircraft circling the airfield at the same time. The SAAF took part with a flight of five Westland Wapitis and their star attraction, six new Hawker Fury fighters. Early in 1936 the SAAF had taken charge of seven Furies (Nos 200-206), which had been assembled at Wynberg in the Cape, and tested on 18 May. They were then flown to Pretoria via Port Elizabeth, enabling them to participate in their first air show. The press reported: 'The Hawker Furies were the limelight of the pageant. Their dazzling display of aerobatics, their speed and power were positively amazing, their response to controls was breathtaking. Perhaps the most astonishing feature of their performance was their ability to do anything without losing height and the remarkably steep angles of climb at speed.'

At the outbreak of World War II the Fury was obsolete, but did see limited action with the SAAF in East Africa. By the time the conflict had begun, the Hawker Hurricane, developed from the Fury, went into action with the SAAF, and for a short period both types served with 1 Squadron. In 1941 a few of the remaining Furies toured the Union with a touring SAAF show called the Air Commando, after which they faded from the scene.

The first fighter purchased by the SAAF since the SE 5As supplied by Britain in 1920, the Hawker Fury (designed by Sydney Camm) resembled the larger Hawker Hart series. Like most Hawker machines it was constructed with a welded steel tubular fuselage girder frame and timber formers and stringers to achieve the sleek, attractive fabric-covered outer shape. All flying surfaces had aluminium spars, timber ribs and fabric covering. The beautifully contoured nose, which was sharply raked from the cockpit, had a metal covering.

Powered by a 525 hp (390 kW) Rolls-Royce Kestrel II engine, which gave it a maximum speed of 207 mph (333 km/h) at 14 000 ft (4 267 m), the Fury I could climb to 10 000 ft (3 048 m) in less than 6 minutes.

Notes on the finish
When delivered, the Furies of the SAAF were Silver overall, apart from the cowlings and metal panels forward of the cockpit, which were highly polished. Roundels were worn on wings and fuselage, but there were no rudder stripes. The serial numbers on the rear fuselage and undersides were repeated on the rudder.

During a memorable display at the opening of the Port Elizabeth (or South End) Aerodrome in 1936, the Hawker Fury I was shown in South Africa for the first time.

Ryan S-T-A

Right: *The Ryan logo painted on the fin of AKP.*

Below: *With a southern storm building in the background, a Ryan S-T-A flies over Port Elizabeth.*

On 8 January 1928 the first air display in Port Elizabeth was held to celebrate the official opening of the Fairview Aerodrome, and on this occasion the Mayor presented the recently-formed Port Elizabeth Light Aeroplanes Club with their first aircraft, a Westland Widgeon (G-UAAH), which was at that stage the only monoplane in the country. The highlight of the occasion was an air race between two de Havilland Moths, an Avro Avian and the Widgeon, flying around the Fairview Seating Stand and the Grey High School clock tower. Unfortunately the club had a short lifespan, as it was liquidated in October 1931 due to a lack of official support.

In June 1936 private flying was re-established with the formation of the Port Elizabeth Aero Club. With government support a number of instructors completed the new Air Force Course at Roberts Heights in order to assist private clubs with a programme of primary training for future SAAF pilots. In January 1937 it was reported that a new Ryan S-T-A would be used by the Port Elizabeth Aero Club for its pilot training scheme, which was introduced that year. In October the first two Ryans were unpacked and assembled at Port Elizabeth, and eventually three (ZS-AKP, ZS-AKU and ZS-ALZ) operated from there. The type was also used at East London by Haller Aviation. At the start of World War II the Ryans were operating as primary trainers, albeit in civil markings. On receiving their wings, pilots transferred to advanced machines like the Westland Wapiti, flown during camps at major bases.

During the war ZS-AKP, ZS-AKU and ZS-ALZ became Nos 1446, 1482 and 1437 respectively when they were taken over by the SAAF, mainly as communications machines.

With its oval metal fuselage, beautifully spatted undercarriage and well-braced Alclad, spruce and fabric wings, the Ryan was an exceptionally attractive aircraft, and young pilots found it difficult to resist. A Menasco C45 150 hp (112 kW) engine gave it a maximum speed of 150 mph (241 km/h) and a ceiling of 17 500 ft (5 334 m).

Notes on the finish
The natural-metal surfaces were well-polished and the fabric surfaces silver-doped. A dark blue fuselage cheatline was worn on two machines. The civil registration letters on Ryan ZS-AKP were applied with an unusual taper.

Fairey Seafox

In 1936 HMS *Amphion* replaced HMS *Dorsetshire* as flagship of the Africa Station and two years later she was transferred to Australia as HMS *Perth*. Serving aboard her replacement, the new HMS *Neptune* (under the command of Vice-Adml G. H. D'Orly Lyon), was a large contingent of South Africans, which made her one of the most popular warships ever stationed in these waters. Sadly the last three Africa Station flagships were all lost during World War II: *Dorsetshire* and *Amphion* (*Perth*) were sunk by the Japanese, while *Neptune* sank after striking four mines in the Mediterranean, with great loss of life.

On the morning of 9 May 1939, however, *Neptune* looked very sleek and attractive as she cleared the harbour entrance on her way out. Suddenly, however, the idyllic scene was rudely shattered. Following the shoreline and flying very low, the ship's Fairey Seafox seaplane, its silver surfaces reflecting the early morning sun, heralded its arrival with a screeching, metallic throb.

A two-bay biplane with folding wings, the two-seater Seafox was the standard spotter-reconnaissance seaplane operated from Royal Navy cruisers. It boasted a smooth semi-monocoque all-metal fuselage and floats, while the flying surfaces were all-metal, with fabric covering. The observer had the luxury of an enclosed cockpit, but the pilot sat in the open to facilitate catapult operations.

The Seafox was fitted with a 395 hp (295 kW) Napier Rapier VI engine, and was capable of 124 mph (200 km/h), with a ceiling of 11 000 ft (3 353 m) and a climb rate of just over 10 minutes to 5 000 ft (1 524 m). Even though the type was structurally considerably more advanced than the Fairey IIIF and Hawker Osprey, its performance was not much better than that of the latter aircraft. Still, during the Battle of the River Plate it was a Seafox from HMS *Ajax* (*Neptune*'s sister) that spotted throughout the action with *Graf Spee*.

Notes on the finish

The finish was Silver overall, including all metal coverings and struts. Seafox K8575 from *Neptune* wore wing and fuselage insignia, but no rudder stripes.

Hawker Hartbees

On a calm, clear morning in May 1939 off the coast near East London passengers aboard the Deutsche Ost-Afrika Linie liner *Pretoria*, racing the Union-Castle mailship *Athlone Castle* to the Buffalo River mouth, were attracted by the sight of three silver aircraft flying in line astern. The sharp exhaust crackle and ringing undertone of their Rolls-Royce Kestrel engines sounded very loud in the early morning calm as the Hawker Hartbees fighter-bombers headed towards Woodbrook Aerodrome after a trial flight prior to the establishment of an Active Citizen Force squadron in East London.

Towards the end of 1939 examples of the Hawker Hartbees and Hawker Hart arrived at East London as the first aircraft to be based in the Eastern Cape for operational training. Because security restrictions had not yet been introduced, the powerful, beautifully-maintained machines with their aircrew in smart white overalls, black flying helmets and weighty parachutes became a public attraction on week-ends.

On 2 February 1940 Eastern Province Command Headquarters moved from East London to Port Elizabeth, and less than six months later the Hartbees was in action against Italian forces in East Africa, with its Silver finish replaced by a camouflage scheme. When replaced by more capable aircraft, they returned to the Union where they were employed as trainers and general-purpose hacks alongside Harts, Hinds and Audaxes. Most ended as scrap before 1944.

A derivative of the Hawker Hart family, and adapted from the Audax, the Hartbees was specifically designed for production in the Union, to be employed in close-support duties in tropical conditions. An initial batch of four examples (Nos 801-804) were delivered by Hawkers, followed by 65 licence-built machines constructed at Roberts Heights. Entering service in 1936, they were augmented in 1938 by 200 secondhand Hart bombers and trainers purchased from Britain at a cost of £200 each – one twelfth of the original production cost.

The Hartbees was powered by a 608 hp (455 kW) Rolls-Royce Kestrel V FB engine. It had a top speed of 176 mph (283 km/h), climbed to 10 000 ft (3 048 m) in 8,4 minutes and had a ceiling of 22 000 ft (6 706 m). Although this performance was slightly lower than that of the Hart, its loaded weight was increased by 270 lb (122 kg).

In the early morning calm in May 1939 near East London a Hawker Hartbees passes over the liners Athlone Castle *and* Pretoria *racing each other to the harbour.*

Notes on the finish

When first commissioned, the Hartbees was Silver overall with a polished metal cowling. Roundels were worn on the wings and fuselage, but there were no fin flashes or rudder stripes. The serial numbers, sometimes accompanied by thin matching bands, were applied to the rear fuselage in Black. In operations the aircraft had Dark Green and Dark Earth upper surfaces with Sky Blue (SAAF 'A') undersides. A, A1 and B roundels with fin flashes were applied, as well as serial numbers in Black.

When originally displayed at the South African National Museum of Military History, the sole remaining Hartbees (No 851) wore its original finish, but subsequently was unfortunately repainted in the present inaccurate scheme.

With the early morning sun reflecting off the sea, a Westland Wapiti flies over the armed auxiliary cruiser Alcantara, *which docked at Port Elizabeth for repairs and increased armament after an engagement with the German raider* Thor.

Westland Wapiti

When the SAAF were looking for a replacement for their well-worked de Havilland 9s, the obvious choice was the Westland Wapiti. A license agreement was consequently arranged with Westland and the first four machines were delivered by the parent company in October 1929. These were followed by the first South African-built example, which flew in April 1931. Although generally superseded by the Hawker Hartbees from 1938 onwards, Wapitis carried out the first routine coastal patrols at the Cape during the early part of World War II. Operating mainly at

dawn and dusk, they flew between Saldanha Bay and Hermanus, but by 1943 nearly all the examples of this reliable workhorse had disappeared.

Designed to replace the DH 9A in the RAF as the standard general-purpose aircraft in the Middle East and India, the Westland Wapiti incorporated as many DH 9A components as possible. By retaining the de Havilland flying surfaces and incorporating a redesigned fuselage and engine (much the same as the design Chance Vought introduced on the UO-1 for the US Navy), a machine with an all-round improvement in performance was built.

The first four examples delivered to South Africa by the parent company were powered by the 550 hp (410 kW) Bristol Jupiter IX F

engine designed by Roy Fedden, but the first South African-built Wapiti flew with an alternative engine, the 525 hp (390 kW) Armstrong Siddeley Panther. The prefix J or P painted with the serial number identified the power plant.

Notes on the finish
The Wapiti had an overall Silver finish with Dark Sea Grey fuselage decking. Standard A-type roundels were applied, but no rudder insignia. The serial number was in Black on the rear fuselage. A number of machines were finished in Dark Green, Dark Earth and Sky Blue (SAAF 'A' or 'B') before they were scrapped.

Junkers Ju 86

A Junkers Ju 86 of 14 Squadron flies on patrol over the Japanese ship Hokoku Maru *in Algoa Bay during the early part of World War II.*

When war with Germany seemed inevitable by June 1939, the SAAF began mobilizing whatever aircraft could be used for military purposes, and the SAA's new Ju 86s were converted to bombers. With open mid-upper gun turrets and exterior bomb racks under the wings, they flew to the coast in October 1939 to be employed on maritime patrol duties.

In support of these operations the Port Elizabeth Municipality agreed to the Department of Defence's occupying ground adjoining the Port Elizabeth Aerodrome in South End for the construction of a large hangar. From January 1940, however, all civil airports were taken over by the Government for the duration of the war, and 13, 14, 15 and 16 Squadrons were based at Durban, Port Elizabeth, Cape Town and Walvis Bay respectively.

The active SAAF Ju 86s had an early success when in December 1939 they intercepted the Deutsche Ost-Afrika Linie liner *Watussi* attempting to return to Germany. Rather than surrender, her captain scuttled the vessel. The fortunes of war are sometimes ironical: in this instance German aircraft serving the Union were instrumental in the sinking of a German ship which for years had served South Africa. Many will remember her and her sister *Ubena*, as both had attractive decor and offered outstanding service.

Shortly after the sinking of the *Watussi*, another irony occurred when patrolling Ju 86s spotted a new shape in Algoa Bay. One of three sister ships built for the South African trade, the Japanese *Hokoku Maru* wore standard Osaka Shosen markings as well as two Japanese flags on each side of her hull to signal her neutrality. Except for her prominent and rather unattractive Sampson Posts, she was very much like the Ellerman Line *City of Port Elizabeth* class passenger ships built in the 1950s. Accommodation and service were also of an exceptional standard. These new ships curtailed their service to the Union shortly before the Japanese attack on Pearl Harbour, but later returned to South African waters under very different circumstances (see p 48).

Early in May 1940, when Avro Anson GRs became available for coastal duties, the Ju 86s were withdrawn, camouflaged and allocated to 12 Squadron for action in East Africa. Accompanying Fairey Battles of 11 Squadron, they carried out the first SAAF operational sorties of World War II – against Italian forces in Ethiopia and Somalia. When replaced by Martin Marylands, they were flown back to the Union and in July 1942 a number were used to initially equip 22 Squadron in Durban until the arrival of their Lockheed Venturas. Thereafter Ju 86s slowly disappeared from the scene, although an overall Silver machine with Blue trim, possibly from 61 Squadron, was seen over Port Elizabeth in early 1945.

An elegant aeroplane, the Ju 86 – designed at a time when many German aircraft were

planned for civil and military roles – was also available as a bomber. When SAA ordered no less than 17 transports, they also took delivery of one Ju 86 K-I bomber, which no doubt was of great help when the transports were converted.

Rolls-Royce Kestrel engines were initially fitted in place of Junkers Jumo 205 diesels to the first five SAA machines, but because the Kestrels were unsuitable for civil operations, 800 hp (600 kW) Pratt & Whitney Hornet radials were later adopted for South African Ju 86s. Their maximum speed was 230 mph (370 km/h) at 10 000 ft (3 048 m).

Although considered obsolete by the Luft-waffe in 1936, the Ju 86, modified for high-altitude work, made a spectacular operational debut. Fitted with special Jumo 207 high-altitude engines, lengthened wings and a pressurised cabin, the Ju 86P flew over the British Isles at 41 000 ft (12 497 m), immune to defence fighters. As spy planes they would climb to maximum altitude and glide over the target area, unheard and often unseen. This situation was redressed with the introduction of the longspan Supermarine Spitfire VII and VIII (see p 74).

Notes on the finish
After conversion to patrol bombers, the coastal Ju 86s retained their SAA paintwork, originally applied in Germany. This was the official German finish for both military and civil aircraft, chosen to replace Silver from 1935. The colour – a pale Grey – had a slight green cast. The SAA Cerullean Blue trim, including the engine nacelles, was retained, as were the three civil registration letters to identify aircraft. SAAF roundels were applied to the fuselage and wings, but there were no fin flashes.

The aircraft serving with 12 Squadron were Dark Green overall with A-type wing roundels, AI roundels on the fuselage and full-height fin flashes. The roundel blue appeared to be SAAF type 'AA'. The large serial numbers were in Black on the rear fuselage. In addition to the overall Silver and Blue 61 Squadron machine, a Dark Green, Dark Earth and dirty Sky Blue machine was also seen in Port Elizabeth.

Vickers Valentia

In March 1940 four large silver twin-engined biplane transport aircraft swept low over East London in close formation, almost resembling yachts with their relatively slow speed, four sets of wheels and masses of rigging. The aircraft were Vickers Valentias, seven of which (Nos 264-270) were delivered to the SAAF from 70 Squadron (RAF) when they were superseded in the Middle East by Vickers Wellesleys. Together with four additional machines (Nos 631-634), they were formed into 50 Transport Squadron at Zwartkop Air Station. Their first undertaking was to fly troops from coastal areas for service in East Africa, and thereafter they served as transports 'up North' until flown back to the Union at the end of 1940. Although obsolete, they were seen in South African skies as general transports until they were retired in late 1942.

Developed from the Vickers Victoria, which equipped 70 and 216 Squadrons of the RAF in Iraq and Egypt, the Valentia was very similar to the late versions of its predecessor. Victorias visited the Union as early as 1931 when 216 Squadron flew from the Middle East to Cape Town on a training flight.

The fabric-covered metal structure of the Valentia had an attractively rounded nose and cabin section of timber semi-monocoque construction. Powered by two 650 hp (485 kW) Bristol Pegasus II engines, the type had a maximum speed of 130 mph (209 km/h), a loaded weight of 19 500 lb (8 775 kg) and could climb at 700 ft/min (213 m/min).

Notes on the finish
The overall Silver finish was soon replaced by the same scheme used by the Junkers Ju 52/3ms. All top surfaces were Dark Green and the undersides Sky Blue (SAAF 'B'). A and AI roundels were applied, while not all machines had fin flashes. Some serial numbers were badly painted in Black, as in the case of No 270. At least one machine had a standard Dark Green, Dark Earth and Sky Blue finish.

Looking for all the world like a large yacht, a Vickers Valentia banks over the Swartkops River before heading eastwards.

Bristol Blenheim I

On 10 June 1940 the Lloyd Triestino round-Africa liners *Timavo* and *Gerusalemme* put to sea from Durban when their captains were secretly informed that war was imminent. Supposedly bound for Cape Town, the two ships in fact steered north for neutral Portuguese waters. A Blenheim I (the only one of its type to serve with the SAAF) attached to 'A' flight of 31 Squadron tracked the ships. When Italy declared war on the night of 11 June, the fully-armed Blenheim took off to intercept the enemy ships.

Timavo was spotted a few miles offshore, but only after bombs were dropped ahead of the ship did her captain react: he altered course and drove the ship ashore at full speed near the mouth of St Lucia Bay. The crew returned to Durban as prisoners of war. *Gerusalemme* escaped under cover of darkness and survived the war, returning to the South African run in 1948.

A Bristol Blenheim I (L1431), the first low-wing all-metal monoplane bomber to serve with the SAAF, was delivered for evaluation towards the end of 1938. It was given the SAAF serial number 401, but became AX683 at the end of 1940, when it was returned to the RAF. Although Blenheim IVs and Bisleys served with 15, 16 and 17 Squadrons overseas, none returned to the Union.

The type first entered service with the RAF in 1937, and at the time it was their fastest bomber, with a top speed of 260 mph (418 km/h). Powered by two 840 hp (630 kW) Bristol Mercury VIII engines, it had a climb rate of 1 540 ft/min (469 m/min) and a range of 1 125 miles (1 811 km). Light to handle, and with an excellent view from the cockpit, the Blenheim I was popular with aircrews but was being replaced by the Mk IV when war broke out. This mark did, however, see service in the Middle East and Greece.

Notes on the finish
Blenheim No 401 was painted in the standard RAF Bomber Command finish of Dark Green and Dark Earth with Black (Night) undersides. It wore A1 and B roundels, but no fin flashes. It retained its original finish until returned to the RAF.

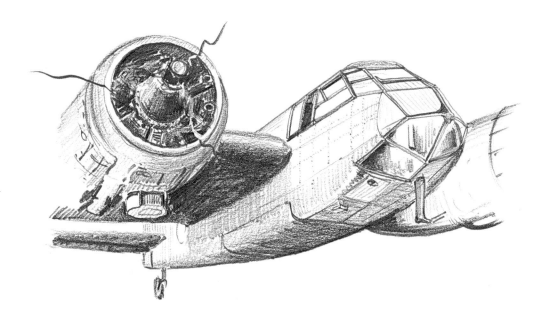

Right: *Detail of the nose of a Bristol Blenheim I.*

Opposite: *A Blenheim flies low over the wreck of the Italian liner* Timavo *on the Zululand coast shortly after she was beached at speed by her captain.*

An Avro Anson GR I of 33 Coastal Reconnaissance
Flight over the Italian refugee repatriation ship
Duilio in Algoa Bay in April 1942.

Avro Anson GR I

While the Junkers Ju 86s were on coastal duties, 13, 14, 15 and 16 Squadrons were redesignated 31 and 32 Coastal Squadrons. The 'A' Flight of 31 Squadron was stationed at Durban, while its 'B' Flight operated from Port Elizabeth. Initially the 'A' Flight of 32 Squadron was stationed at Cape Town and its 'B' Flight at Walvis Bay, but during June 1940 'B' Flight returned to Cape Town where it was combined with 'A' Flight. On 1 September 1940 the coastal units were again redesignated, this time as Coastal Reconnaissance Flights, with 31 CRF at Cape Town, 32 CRF at Durban and 33 CRF at Port Elizabeth.

By this time the Ju 86s of 33 CRF had been replaced by new Avro Anson GR Is, and the unit occupied a large new hangar on the southern side of the Port Elizabeth Airfield (see p 94). With the Ansons came the typical unsynchronized throb of their twin 350 hp (260 kW) Armstrong Siddeley Cheetah IX engines, a sound which was to be heard regularly, day and night, until after World War II.

Apart from routine patrols, 33 CRF were called on to carry out a deepsea search for the German raider *Pinquin* off the coast during August and September 1940. In March 1941 the pocket battleship *Admiral Scheer* was reported off the coast, and again 33 CRF flew south to the limit of their range. However, the warship passed 500 miles south of the Cape and escaped detection.

In April 1942 33 CRF monitored the movements of four interesting ships. Two of these, the sisters *Duilio* and *Giulio Cesare* (popular Lloyd Triestino liners on the South African run before the war), and a second pair, the *Saturnia* and *Vulcania*, sailed into Algoa Bay for stores and bunkers. Although they sailed under the flag of an Axis power, they were allowed free passage, as they were refugee carriers en route to East Africa to repatriate some of the 18 000 Italian women, children and non-combatants trapped in the former Italian colony of Abyssinia. Painted white overall, with large red crosses and Italian flags on their hulls, the ships looked impressive. Sad-ly both *Duilio* and *Giulio Cesare*, still wearing these markings, were sunk in Trieste in 1944 by rocket-firing Bristol Beaufighters of the RAF and SAAF.

In July 1942, shortly before the formation of 25 Squadron (equipped with Lockheed B-34 Venturas), 33 CRF was disbanded. (A few of 33 CRF's Ansons and their crews formed part of 25 Squadron when that unit was formed in Port Elizabeth.) It may have been a small flight, but it had pioneered wartime service flying in Port Elizabeth. From 1941 it became closely related to 42 Air School, whose expansion was centered on the 'old' hangar.

The Avro Anson was a military version of the Avro 652 (derived from the Fokker Avro 10) to which was added a gun turret, forward-firing gun and capacity to carry a limited bomb load. The GR I was built for general reconnaissance, and was delivered to the Union for coastal patrols. The Anson had a range of 790 miles (1 271 km) while cruising at 158 mph (254 km/h), which certainly did not qualify it as a long-range maritime aircraft, but it was reliable and structurally safe.

Of conventional construction, the welded steel tubular-framed fuselage had formers and stringers with fabric covering, and the flying surfaces had plywood skinning over their timber structures. A chain-driven screw gear retracted the undercarriage (this required 140 turns) – a system disliked by aircrews, and probably the reason why many trainer Ansons flew with their wheels detracted.

Notes on the finish
The Avro Anson GRs had Dark Green and Dark Earth upper surfaces with Sky Blue (SAAF 'A') undersides. Although camouflaged, A-type roundels were applied to upper and lower surfaces, with A1 fuselage insignia and full fin flashes, as well as White code letters. The Black serial numbers appeared only on the rear fuselage.

The emblem of 33 Coastal Reconnaisance Flight.

The emblem of 42 Air School.

Junkers Ju 52/3m

When South African Airways was formed by the take-over of Union Airways, the new company took control of all UA's aircraft, including three new Junkers Ju 52/3ms on order. On 16 November 1934, not long after their delivery to the Union, the first of these (ZS-AFA, 'Jan van Riebeeck'), arrived over Port Elizabeth. Because the Fairview Aerodrome was too small for the 'Giant Junkers – Monarch of the Skies' as the press dubbed her, she landed at Uitenhage after circling Port Elizabeth.

On the outbreak of World War II SAA's eleven Ju 52/3ms were taken over by the SAAF for service with 50 Squadron to shuttle troops and supplies to East Africa. They were regularly seen at air stations in the Union and one, No 666 (formerly ZS-ALO, also named 'Jan van Riebeeck'), was a Pratt & Whitney Hornet-powered replacement for ZS-AFA which, with the other two BMW-powered machines, had been resold to Junkers. After the war they disappeared from service – including one which was displayed at the South African National Museum of Military History until it was disposed of, together with a number of other valuable aircraft, in the early 1950s.

A Junkers Ju 52/3m flying over the Valley of Desolation near Graaff-Reinet en route to Bloemfontein from George.

Built as a successor to a well-established line of transports, the Ju 52/3m, derived from the original Ju 52 cargo transport (which was powered by a single 755 hp (565 kW) BMW VII A), became one of the most significant pre-war airliners and also the transport mainstay of the Luftwaffe during World War II. Powered by three BMW 132 A or Pratt & Whitney Hornet engines, it was constructed with the standard Junkers corrugated skinning known as Duralumin (an aluminium and copper alloy) which was created by the Düren Metallwerke company for the construction of Zeppelins.

Notes on the finish
In SAAF service the Junkers Ju 52/3ms had mainly Matt Dark Green upper surfaces and SAAF Sky Blue 'B' undersides. The serial numbers were Black and sometimes a Yellow code letter was worn. A, A1 and B roundels and full-height fin flashes were worn. A few machines had Dark Green and Dark Earth upper surfaces. An interesting example was No 662 'B' which had faded Dark Green upper surfaces which included areas around the engines repainted with darker fresh paint darkened even further by exhaust marks and patches of gloss from oil spread by mechanics over the wing upper surfaces. The underside roundels were of a non-standard D type.

HMTS *Orbita*

In October 1939 the Empire Air Training Scheme was launched with the aim of including the Dominions in an overall aircrew training programme. South Africa, however, decided not to participate because it was felt that training should be completed in the Union, whereas the EATS envisaged that advanced training would be completed in Canada. By January 1940 the EATS had begun in Canada and Australia, where thousands of aspiring airmen were in the making.

On 11 April 1940 Gen Smuts revealed that the British Government had accepted the Union's offer to afford training facilities for aircrews. Known as the Joint Air Training Scheme, it would, apart from training RAF crews, allow the latest methods to be adopted by the SAAF. Air Chief Marshal Sir Robert Brooke Popham, who assisted with the inauguration of the EATS, came to the Union to co-ordinate the scheme. As a result three groups were formed, with 25 Group centered on the Eastern Cape. This Group comprised 42 Air School and 11 Operational Training Unit ('B' Squadron) at Port Elizabeth, 41 and 48 AS at East London, 43 AS at Port Alfred, 44 AS at Grahamstown, 47 AS at Queenstown, 45 AS at Oudtshoorn, and 61 AS at George.

The RAF personnel for 42 Air School (28 Draft), left Liverpool in December 1940 aboard HMTS *Orbita*, a 15 678-ton former passenger ship of the Pacific Steam Navigation Co which had also served as a troopship during World War I. Having endured a long voyage through U-boat-infested waters, as well as a close encounter with the cruiser *Admiral Hipper*, *Orbita* entered Algoa Bay in January 1941. Instead of the expected jungle and savages, the recruits found a picturesque city shimmering in the warm early morning light, and as they entered the harbour, the '1940 British Settlers' heard the bells of the Campanile, church and clock towers ringing across the calm sea. Thereafter RAF personnel often referred to Port Elizabeth as the City of Bells.

HMTS Orbita *off Port Elizabeth on a calm, warm January morning in 1941, with the pilot launch* St Croix *coming alongside.*

Airspeed Oxford

When the new 42 Air School hangars, administration buildings, radio station and camp were erected, they engulfed the 33 Flight hangar and transformed the Port Elizabeth Airfield into a true military air base. Avro Ansons, Airspeed Oxfords, Northrop Nomads and Fairy Battles had arrived — the latter in their Bomber Command combat colours.

About 500 Oxfords served in the Union during the war. Initially they were in the majority at 42 AS, but gradually their numbers were reduced, with the result that by April 1945 Ansons dominated the scene. Training in air navigation, bombing and air gunnery were the main activities at 42 AS. While a few Oxford Is with Armstrong Whitworth gun turrets were in evidence, most were Mk Is with the turrets removed, or Mk IIs. Because Oxfords operated together with Ansons, comparisons were inevitable. The smaller, aesthetically pleasing Oxford appeared the faster, and although the engines of the two types were almost identical, the Oxford's purring beat (rather like a large diesel bus at speed) differed from the Anson's uneven throb.

The Airspeed Oxford story began in 1936. With a new generation of multi-engined monoplane bombers under construction, the British Air Ministry required an advanced twin-engined monoplane trainer. A comparatively

Above: With its Lycoming engine emitting a clattering throb, the Aeronca Chief housed in 33 Coastal Reconnaisance Flight's hangar (which can be seen surrounded by the buildings of 42 Air School, still under construction) climbs over the Port Elizabeth Airfield at dusk.

Right: Captain Nick Carter in 1977.

Aeronca 50c Chief

When 28 Draft arrived at their new home — the Port Elizabeth Airfield at South End — 33 Flight's hangar was the only completed structure, although new hangars were in the process of being erected to house 42 Air School. Their aircraft had not yet arrived, though, so for the first two months, apart from the morning parade, the men were free to spend the days lazing on Humewood Beach.

Flight Officer Fletcher, however, arranged to make use of an Aeronca 50c Chief housed in the corner of 33 Flight's hangar. This was

the station's first meteorological flight (the second was flown by Flight Officer Nick Carter), and took nearly two hours to reach 12 000 feet (3 658 m), not far short of the aircraft's ceiling.

In March 1940 the Aeronca was impressed into the SAAF together with all other civil aircraft, and was attached to 33 Flight as the unit's communications machine.

Notes on the finish
The Aeronca had an overall Silver finish, A-type roundels, fin flashes and Black serial numbers. Some Aeroncas also displayed Black cheat lines.

small and new company, Airspeed, were invited to build such a machine mainly because of their extensive experience with retractable undercarriages. The all-timber Oxford, a development of the Envoy, had wings with box spars and plywood covering. Unlike the Anson, however, the fuselage was built in two sections with a semi-monocoque construction and glued joints. It had one of the best cockpit layouts of its kind, but nevertheless the 'Ox Box' had to be treated with respect, while the Anson was rather tame. Two 370 hp (275 kW) Armstrong Siddeley Cheetah X engines developed a maximum speed of 188 mph (303 km/h) and made possible a climb rate of 960 ft/min (293 m/min).

Notes on the finish

The first Oxfords delivered to South Africa were finished in Dark Green and Dark Earth, with Yellow undersides. Engine cowlings were usually all Dark Green. The Red in the standard RAF A, A1 and B roundels and fin flashes were replaced by SAAF Orange. The illustration of No 3667 shows the neat application of the serial number on the undersides, which tended to become patchy, displaying varying shades of Yellow.

Right: *Contrasted against a stormy sky, an Airspeed Oxford of 42 Air School banks over the former luxury liner* Ile de France, *which was converted to a troopship in Port Elizabeth in 1943.*

Below: *An Oxford burning after ground-looping in 1944.*

Avro Anson

An Avro Anson approaching the Port Elizabeth Airfield in thick fog late in 1943 aborts the landing and goes round again to avoid the wreckage of an Oxford which crashed shortly before. Note the incorrectly applied underside serial number.

Although originally built for the coastal reconnaissance role, the Avro Anson's chief wartime achievement was as a trainer. Initially Anson GR Is had to be transferred to RAF training schools due to a shortage of Airspeed Oxfords. Most of the Anson trainers delivered to South Africa were without turrets and port gun troughs, which were covered. A number were, however, fitted with a Bristol I turret similar to that on the Bristol Blenheim.

Nicknamed 'Annie', the Anson performed remarkably well as a trainer, weekend taxi and general communications hack. During 1942, when the number of sinkings by U-boats along the South African coast increased alarmingly, Ansons from 42 Air School joined in coastal patrols and emergencies, and their engines could be heard revving at all hours when called out. On one such occasion, while the aircraft were out, a heavy mist rolled in off the sea, with the result that when they returned, they alarmed Walmer residents by circling at tree-top level in search of the airfield, from where red flares occasionally penetrated the mist. The following day two Ansons were found nestling in the trees and bushes near the airfield, while another was seen to be resting on its belly near the boundary fence.

In the early hours of 31 October 1942 an Anson (No 3294) struck the corrugated iron roof of a Walmer dwelling shortly after take-off, and both aircraft and roof ended up on the opposite side of the road. One of its wheels landed on a little girl's bed, but fortunately for all concerned she had been sleeping in her parents' room that night because she was suffering from tooth-ache, and as a consequence the accident did not result in any loss of life. Anson No 3294 was later repaired and put back into service (see p 84).

During 1947 the Department of Defence disposed of all surplus aircraft at various bases. In Port Elizabeth scores of Ansons, Oxfords, Hawker Hurricanes and Curtiss Kittyhawks were sold for between £10 and £20 each. A few Ansons served with the SAAF in the post-war years, mainly in a tsetse-fly spraying program. No complete Anson exists in the Republic at present, but the SAAF Museum is involved in a long-term reconstruction project.

Later machines had smooth Oxford-type engine cowlings in place of the characteristic helmeted shape, as well as Vokes filters, which were essential to cope with dust, especially during the dry winters that are a feature of the Highveld.

Notes on the finish
The original Ansons were finished in the standard Dark Green, Dark Earth and Yellow scheme. Many of the later deliveries wore B, C and C1 roundels with matching fin flashes. The two-letter code in White aft of the fuselage roundel was repeated on the sides of the nose. A common sight was numerous odd patches of red tautening dope used to repair holed fabric covering.

R BELLING © 85

Fairey Battle

Still wearing their battle finish after action in Europe, Fairey Battles stationed at 42 Air School introduced Port Elizabethans to the powerful droning crackle of the Rolls-Royce Merlin engine. Battle K9402 was test-flown in April 1939 by the SAAF for evaluation as a possible replacement for their Hawker light bomber force. When more Battles arrived from Britain, they joined K9402, which bore the SAAF serial number 901, for service with 12 Squadron in East Africa, where they operated with success against the Italian forces.

About 150 ex-RAF combat machines were sent to the Union for training purposes and by April 1941 there were approximately 30 in

Port Elizabeth. These effectively operated as bomber trainers, but by early 1943 were mainly employed as target tugs. One example of the trainer version of the Battle (with two separate cockpits) was regularly seen at the base (see p 41).

Representing a great advance over the biplane Hawker Harts and Hawker Hinds when delivered to the RAF, the Fairey machine employed the latest methods of construction. Powered by 1 030 hp (770 kW) Merlin I, II, III or V engines, the Battle was the first service aircraft fitted with this remarkable power plant, which gave it a maximum speed of 240 mph (386 km/h). The Fairey company's first product with a stressed-skin covering, it was a robust machine, and easy to fly.

Although obsolescent by the time World War II broke out, the RAF took Battles to France in 1940 as part of the Advanced Air

Striking Force. They were badly mauled by the Luftwaffe, and, due to unacceptable losses, were withdrawn for training and target tug duties.

Notes on the finish
The first Battles with 42 Air School were finished in Dark Green, Dark Earth and Black (Night), with B and A1 roundels. Some wore full fin flashes or the standard rectangle, while others had a distorted version to line up with the rudder separation. Apart from the rear fuselage serial number, some machines had a single pale Grey or White identification letter, and others a coupled number and letter. On the twin-cockpit trainer the Yellow underside separation was applied along the fuselage centreline.

On a crisp, calm winter's night, a Fairey Battle prepares to take off on a bombing exercise.

Northrop A-17A Nomad

A Northrop Nomad lines up to land at the Port Elizabeth Airfield in October 1942. Along the north boundary are a number of Lockheed B-34 Venturas. Below, the narrow-gauge train which served the farming community west of Port Elizabeth clatters past Victoria Park.

The Northrop A-17A Nomad, a comparatively rare machine, operated for a few years in large numbers from Port Elizabeth, East London and George. Ninety-three of the 170 Nomads supplied to the US Army were, after a year and a half, returned for re-sale to Britain in June 1940. Most of these were redirected to South Africa.

While operational in Port Elizabeth, where they were formed into 'B' Flight at 42 Air School, they served in the air-to-air gunnery target tug role, and monopolised the airspace over the airfield while dropping their targets. When approaching, the Nomad had an engine note which rasped, somewhat like a Harvard, but once overhead, the harsh sound gave way to a soft growling moan which quietly diminished as it flew off. With monotonous regularity they flew over the airfield at between 500 and 700 feet (152 and 213 m), each towing a yellow sleeve drogue target disengaged by a fresh folded drogue which opened with a puff of chalk after having travelled

A Northrop Nomad lines up to land at the Port Elizabeth Airfield in October 1942. Along the north boundary are a number of Lockheed B-34 Venturas. Below, the narrow-gauge train which served the farming community west of Port Elizabeth clatters past Victoria Park.

along the towing cable. In March 1944 'B' Flight was disbanded, however, and the Nomad disappeared from our skies.

A development of the fixed-undercarriage A-17, the A-17A was a two-seater light attack bomber powered by a 825 hp (615 kW) Pratt & Whitney Twin Wasp Junior engine. Of an all-metal construction with Alclad stressed-skin covering, it had characteristic three-piece perforated flaps which could clearly be seen when the Nomad came in low over the boundary fence. Incidentally, the famous Douglas Dauntless – fitted with similar flaps – was conceived as the Northrop BT-1. With a maximum speed of 221 mph (356 km/h), the Nomad climbed at 1 500 ft/min (457 m/min).

Notes on the finish

Although a few Northrop Nomads were Yellow overall with diagonal Black stripes, most were finished in Dark Green and Dark Earth with the Black and Yellow diagonally-striped undersides specified for target tugs. Some, however, had overall Yellow undersides, and one was seen with natural metal wings. A, A1 and B roundels were worn, as well as fin flashes. Most aircraft displayed only their rear fuselage serial number, but some had large Pale Grey numbers or a letter-and-number combination. Although well used, their matt finish was in good condition.

A Northrop Nomad has just disengaged a used drogue, while a Fairey Battle trainer prepares to take off. Note the machine in the background, on its way to the gunnery range after having released a drogue which is drifting over the airfield boundary.

Ground crew refuelling an Avro 504 in the 1920s.

Seconds from destruction, this Avro Tutor flies low over the Baakens River on 23 November 1942. The suburb of South End can be seen in the left background, with Fort Frederick on the opposite side of the valley, while a narrow-gauge locomotive passes the old harbour power station in the foreground.

Avro Tutor

In September 1941 a touring SAAF show known as the Air Commando held air displays throughout the Union. At East London the opening item of 'Crazy Flying' was an outstanding aerobatic performance by Capt Morphew flying in an overall Yellow Avro Tutor. What impressed most was a display of inverted flying over thousands of spectators at a dangerously low altitude.

Having served mainly at Central Flying School during pre-war years, the Tutor was relegated to miscellaneous tasks when the wartime Joint Air Training Scheme was introduced. No 701, the first example delivered from Britain, served with 42 Air School, where it gained notoriety for 'dangerous flying', ie flying over the harbour and performing tight turns between the cranes in exercises with anti-aircraft gunners at the port.

At 10h15 on 23 November 1942, while flying back to the airfield after completing a routine flight, this Tutor struck the roof of a fish processing factory and burst into flames. One of the two aircrew, Lt Lindsay-Rae, survived. He later served on Bristol Beaufighters with 19 Squadron in the Mediterranean, and in postwar years became the Deputy Airport Manager at Port Elizabeth.

By 1944 all Tutors had been struck off charge, including a few at 42 AS which were broken up.

These attractive aircraft, incorporating a steel tubular basic fuselage frame, and powered by a 240 hp (180 kW) Armstrong Siddeley Lynx IVc engine, were chosen to succeed the Avro 504 trainer in the RAF. The SAAF also selected it as their basic trainer, and bought two machines from Avro, whereafter 49 examples were built under licence, starting in 1935.

Notes on the finish
In their heyday at Central Flying School the Tutors were Silver, but during their war service they had a Yellow overall finish. For some unknown reason most had D-type roundels, overall fin flashes and large Black fuselage serial numbers.

Hawker Audax

In addition to the South African-built Hawker Hartbees and more than 200 Hawker Harts bought from Britain in 1938, approximately 170 Hawker Hinds and 75 Hawker Audaxes were sent to the Union as they became surplus to RAF requirements, beginning in 1940. Many of these army co-operation versions of the Hart were issued to Air Schools for general-purpose duties. At 42 Air School, for example, there were five Audaxes, two Harts and two Hinds.

When on meteorological flights, they usually flew from east to west at about 10 000 ft (3 000 m). During calm late afternoons the low sun coloured their Yellow undersides with tints of pink and orange. A sudden flash and ball of smoke would appear not far behind the aircraft and a few seconds later a report would be heard above the distant crackle of the Rolls-Royce Kestrel engine. The puffs of smoke were an aid in measuring drift, and were an important requirement for night-bombing training flights.

By early 1944 the Hawker biplanes – replaced by Airspeed Oxfords on the meteorological flights – were broken up in Port Elizabeth and the remains buried.

Notes on the finish

While the Hawker Audaxes were finished in Dark Green and Dark Earth with Yellow undersides, some Harts and Hinds were Yellow overall. A, A1 and B roundels with overall fin flashes were worn. Black serial numbers were confined to the rear fuselage.

R BELLING © 84

Its Yellow undersides tinted pink and orange by the late afternoon sun, a Hawker Audax flies over the Port Elizabeth Airfield after having released a smoke marker as an aid in measuring wind drift.

De Havilland 82A Tiger Moth

The de Havilland 82A Tiger Moth, the most famous primary trainer to serve with the SAAF, equipped the elementary flying schools (24 Group) during World War II. Based mainly in the Transvaal and Orange Free State, the 'Tiger' seldom operated from Port Elizabeth, but occasionally one or two called at 42 Air School. Shortly after the war, however, more than a hundred Tiger Moths arrived at Port Elizabeth, usually in flights of four, to be stripped and shipped overseas.

In the early post-war years the Tiger Moth came into its own again when the SAAF reintroduced Active Citizen Force flying training during the early 1950s, and flying clubs used Tiger Moths as primary trainers. Pilots who qualified continued their flying training in North American Harvards with Citizen Force squadrons such as 6 Squadron 'City of Port Elizabeth' (see pp 57 and 114).

The Tiger Moth was always an aesthetically pleasing and graceful sight. The attractive moth-shaped tail surfaces, inherited from its predecessors (the Moth, Gipsy Moth, Moth Trainer and Moth Major), were the company's hallmark. The welded steel tubular fuselage framing had plywood decking, while flying surfaces were timber-structured, with fabric covering. A 130 hp (97 kW) DH Gipsy Major engine was fitted.

Notes on the finish
Although not recorded at 42 Air School, early DH Tiger Moths should have been finished in the standard RAF Dark Green, Dark Earth, and Yellow sheme, but in the Union overall Yellow became standard. Before the end of World War II, C-type roundels became more common, but A roundels were the standard type, although occasionally the D type was seen. Sky Blue (SAAF 'A') replaced the correct Insignia Blue on a number of machines. Fuselage serial numbers were usually large, but a few aircraft retained their earlier small numbers. The usual full fin flashes were overpainted Yellow in some cases. A variety of yellows was used on different components, as was often the case on Avro Ansons and Airspeed Oxfords.

With its engine making a popping sound, a de Havilland Tiger Moth comes in to land at the Port Elizabeth Airfield. In the background the trees of Victoria Park add tranquillity to the idyllic pastoral spring scene.

R BELLINC © 83

De Havilland 85 Leopard Moth

One of seven de Havilland 85 Leopard Moths impressed into the SAAF, ZS-AEJ became No 1407, and while serving with 61 Squadron it visited Port Elizabeth from George on communications duties.

Designed as a luxury 3-seater private aircraft in 1933 to succeed the DH 80 Puss Moth, which it closely resembled, the Leopard Moth, powered by a 130 hp (97 kW) DH Gipsy Major engine, had typical graceful de Havilland lines. To save weight, the fuselage was built as a box structure of spruce and plywood with stringers and an outer fabric finish instead of the welded steel frame of the Puss Moth. The timber-framed flying surfaces were fabric-covered.

Notes on the finish
Although an overall Yellow scheme was used on impressed machines, most communications types appeared in the more practical Silver finish, usually with Red, Black or Blue trim. No 1407, finished in the latter scheme, had a Red nose, wheel covers and an animated 61 Squadron crest on the nose. A-type roundels with full fin flashes were worn, and the wingstruts were Black. The insignia blue was SAAF Roundel Blue 'AA'.

Sedately cruising over the Swartkops River on a balmy Saturday early in 1943, a de Havilland Leopard Moth heads towards the river mouth.

Douglas A-20 Boston III

On 8 May 1942 a Douglas A-20 Boston III circled Port Elizabeth with a powerful roar from its 1 600 hp (1 200 kW) double-row Wright Cyclone engines. One of the latest combat aircraft to serve with the SAAF, this Boston was specially withdrawn from operations with 12 Squadron in North Africa to tour the Union on a recruiting campaign. It was flown by Capt Visser, and also on board was Lt-Col Hartshorn, DSO, who lectured on the tour, which had the same objective as that of Maj Miller in 1917 (see p 9).

In the SAAF, 24 Squadron (and later 12 Squadron as well) replaced their Martin Marylands with the Boston III (which they operated against the Afrika Corps) in December 1941 and March 1942 respectively. However, during what was called 'Boston Tea Parties' they met very strong opposition from Lufwaffe Messerschmitt Bf 109s.

Somewhat of an improvement over the Bristol Blenheim IV which it replaced, the Douglas machine was very popular with its crews. The RAF used theirs for daylight raids over France and the Low Countries, and it also served the United States in Europe and the Far East. The best-known American bomber to serve with the RAF in World War II, and the first with a tricycle undercarriage, the Boston was a three-seater light bomber with a top speed of 304 mph (489 km/h). It could carry a bomb load of 2 000 lb (900 kg) and had a range of 1 020 miles (1 642 km).

Notes on the finish
When delivered to the RAF, most Bostons were finished in Dark Green and Dark Earth with Sky undersides – the standard day-bomber scheme. In the case of aircraft operating in the Middle East the Dark Green was overpainted with Middle Stone according to Air Ministry Directive AMO A 926/40. Although officially introduced only later, Azure Blue replaced the Sky undersides. Roundels were of the B and AI type, with standard fin flashes, while the White code letter positioned aft of the fuselage roundel was repeated in a smaller version aft of the nose glazing.

Left: *A message roughly painted on the side of a Douglas Boston used for recruiting purposes.*

Opposite: *Contrasting strongly against the sea along the Southern Cape coast, a Boston of 12 Squadron circles the Italian refugee ships* Vulcania *and* Saturnia *in 1942.*

ward of the conning tower which accommodated type A midget submarines designed to penetrate harbour defences.

The flagship, No I-IO, also carried a Yokosuka E14Y reconnaissance seaplane (codenamed 'Glen' by the Allies). Serving with 932 Naval Air Group, the machines were distributed to various ships to be flown over ports at dawn or at night to ascertain whether major naval targets were at anchor. If there were, an attack by the midget submarines would be implemented. Such scouting flights were flown between 20-27 April over South African ports, but fortunately no potential targets were sighted.

On 29 April, however, the Glen on board I-IO spotted a Queen Elizabeth-class battleship and tanker at anchor in Diego Suarez. Midget type A submarines from I-18 and I-20 attacked and badly damaged HMS *Ramillies* and sank the tanker, and only after nearly a year in Durban's dry-dock was *Ramillies* able once more to put to sea. It is interesting to note that *Hokoku Maru* (see p 28), an 'armed merchant cruiser' was the general support vessel for 8th Submarine Squadron units in South African waters.

A two-seater twin-float seaplane powered by a 300/340 hp (225/255 kW) Hitachi Tempu 12 9-cylinder air-cooled engine, the E14Y had a welded steel tubular structure covered with fabric. The light-alloy floats were removable and the wings folded for easy stowage. With a speed of 153 mph (246 km/h) and a range of 550 miles (885 km), the Glen operated only in calm weather.

An impression of a Yokosuka E14Y 'Glen' circling Port Elizabeth in the early morning light before returning to its mother submarine somewhere at sea.

Yokosuka E14Y 'Glen'

During the early morning hours of 22 April 1942 an unidentified aircraft flew over Port Elizabeth, and although none of the 42 Air School aircraft were able to intercept the intruder, it is safe to assume that it was a Japanese Yokosuka E14Y 'Glen' scoutplane. At that time the Japanese controlled most of the Far East, and were extending their activities further west, and in April 1942 five large submarines of the 8th Submarine Squadron under the command of Vice-Adml Ishizaki left Penang for operations along the east coast of Africa and the coast of South Africa. The submarines of this squadron were Nos I-IO, I-16, I-18, I-20 and I-30, all large I-15 class boats equipped with a cylindrical hangar for-

Notes on the finish
According to Japanese records the standard finish for reconnaissance floatplanes was Black Green (N1) for all upper surfaces, which was slightly paler and with a suggestion of Blue as compared to RLM 70. The undersides were Pale Grey (N10), which was somewhat like Medium Sea Grey. The Hinomaru insignia and propeller warning stripes were dark Red. In addition to the standard Black engine cowling and Yellow leading edge stripes, the number 32 of 932 NAG was painted in Yellow on the fin, with the aircraft number on the rudder.

Curtiss P-36 Mohawk IV

In 1938 the Curtiss P-36 was the standard fighter of the United States Army Air Corps. Large orders were also placed by the French Armée de l'Air, but many of these machines were delivered to the RAF after the collapse of France in June 1940. A number of these Mk IV types were in turn redirected to the SAAF, which urgently required modern fighters. From mid-1941 the Mohawks operated in East Africa, with a fair degree of success. With the formation of 3 Squadron later that year Mohawks formed part of its complement, as they did in the case of 4 Squadron.

Early in 1942 most of the Mohawks returned to the Union. With the possibility of Japanese attacks against South African ports looming large, coastal fighter squadrons were established. Reformed with Mohawks during February 1942, 6 Squadron was stationed at Durban, but when the Japanese Navy was confined further east during 1943, the squadron was disbanded and the Mohawk disappeared from the local scene.

Powered by a 1 200 hp (900 kW) Wright Cyclone GR-1820 engine in place of the Pratt & Whitney Wasp fitted to the I, II and III

marks, the Mohawk had a speed of 300 mph (483 km/h), which was less than that of the Douglas Boston. However, the typical Curtiss fighter shape made them look impressive when taking off – with the engine creating a whining roar and the undercarriage turning through 90° while retracting backwards.

Notes on the finish
When delivered to the SAAF the Mohawks were finished in the standard RAF day-fighter scheme of Dark Green, Dark Earth and Sky with A, A1 and B roundels. The Sky was later overpainted with SAAF Sky Blue 'B', and apart from the serial number, a White code letter was carried aft of the fuselage roundel.

A Curtiss Mohawk of 6 Squadron above a heavy sunlit cloudscape.

R BELLIN © 85

North American Harvard I

An aircraft that for many years was an integral part of the South African aviation scene arrived somewhat discreetly in the Union during 1940 when two of three ex-RAF Harvard Is (Nos 1301 and 1302) delivered to South Africa were transferred to the newly-formed 6 Squadron, which was then equipped with Curtiss Mohawks.

Developed from the fixed-undercarriage North American BT-9, the North American 16, powered by the 600 hp (450 kW) Pratt & Whitney Wasp R-1340 engine, had a welded steel tubular-framed fuselage with stringered formers and fabric covering. The all-metal wings had rounded tips, and the rudder an elliptical shape. With a maximum speed of 205 mph (330 km/h), a climb rate of 1 350 ft/min (411 m/min) and a range of 750 miles (1 207 km), the Harvard I became a popular, reliable trainer throughout the Commonwealth, although only three joined the SAAF. In Rhodesia they served alongside Harvard IIs until 1945.

Notes on the finish
Originally delivered in an overall Yellow finish, the RAF machines in Britain adopted the standard trainer scheme of Dark Green and Dark Earth with Yellow undersides, with the separation along the fuselage centreline. The SAAF retained their overall Yellow finish, but the metal nose panels, individual letter ahead of the fuselage roundels, fin flashes and rudder serial numbers were overpainted in a darker Yellow which was accentuated because the original colour had faded. Orange replaced the Red in the A-type roundels, and the new SAAF serial number was painted in Black. Although they retained their RAF serial numbers, the Rhodesian Harvard Is had an individual number in Red below the rear cockpit, repeated on the upper surfaces of the wings, while the serial number appeared on the undersides. By 1945 C-type roundels replaced the A type.

A North American Harvard I in a shallow dive through low raincloud.

Junkers F 13

During 1942-1943 the oldest aeroplane in the SAAF occasionally called at 42 Air School. This was a Junkers F 13 impressed into service as No 259 ('Hendrik Swellengrebel'), the personal aircraft of Col J. Louw, General Officer Commanding Coastal Area.

The type had an historical background which can be said to have started in 1914, when Junkers pioneered the then novel technique of an all-metal construction for aircraft. By the end of World War I the Junkers company had developed an operational low-wing monoplane fighter. Using this experience, the Junkers F 13, arguably the world's first purpose-built airliner, went into production in 1919. Setting a new standard in airline travel with the comfort of an enclosed heated cabin, they were acquired by a good many airlines and remained in production until the early 1930s.

In April 1930 an F 13 displayed at the Johannesburg Agricultural Show impressed Maj Allister Miller, who ordered three examples for Union Airways on condition that they be fitted with British engines. The first example, assembled at Port Elizabeth in January 1932, had an Armstrong Siddeley Jaguar radial engine, while the remaining pair, flown out from the Junkers factory at Dessau in Germany to Port Elizabeth the following year, were powered by Armstrong Siddeley Pumas.

Junkers were also interested in an airline in South Africa and assisted with the formation of South West African Airways, later to merge with Union Airways. Ultimately, when South African Airways was formed, both companies' F 13s were taken over. 'Hendrik Swellengrebel', one of the original SWAA machines, was impressed into the SAAF as a communications type, and possibly served until 1944.

Notes on the finish
Junkers F 13 No 259 had a protective Silver finish with the cowling, undercarriage structure and serial number in Black. A-type roundels were worn only on the wings.

Lockheed B-34 Ventura

Opposite: A Lockheed B-34 Ventura of 25 Squadron passes a convoy in rough weather outside Algoa Bay while the escort HMS Northern Duke *pitches through a heavy swell.*

Below: Another 25 Squadron Ventura on patrol over the forward section of the United States Liberty ship Anne Hutchinson, *under tow to Port Elizabeth. Torpedoed in October 1942 off East London, she broke in two and drifted westward until found off Port Alfred.*

The Port Elizabeth Airfield underwent further development during 1942. Formed in 1941 as SAAF maintenance units, 7 and 12 Air Depots were temporarily accommodated in hangars at 42 Air School while what was virtually a new air station, referred to as 7 Air Depot (or Driftsands), was built on the east side of the base, with comprehensive workshops, hangars and test facilities to service 42 AS aircraft as well as machines based at the new, three-runway military airfield under construction at St Albans, 16 miles west of Port Elizabeth.

During 1942, when sinkings by U-boats increased along the South African coast, training units like 42 AS had to undertake patrols. New airfields were hastily constructed at Darling, Rooikop (near Walvis Bay), Bredasdorp, St Albans, Lombazi and Mtubatuba for the new Lockheed Ventura units which were planned to be up to strength in 1943, thus enabling the training schools to return to normal conditions. The number of ships sunk by U-boats in South African waters totalled 5 in 1939, 4 in 1940, 7 in 1941, 81 in 1942, 49 in 1943, 8 in 1944 and 1 in 1945.

In July 1942 33 Flight was disbanded, to be replaced by 25 Squadron, one of the new Ventura units. Although Bristol Beauforts were intended to replace the Avro Ansons then in use, only nine of the expected 35 arrived and these were not equipped to carry torpedoes. However, fairly large numbers of Lockheed B-34 Venturas were due to equip the new coastal patrol units, one of which was 25 Squadron, formed at Port Elizabeth in September 1942. During October 1942 three of the new Venturas were seen over Humewood Beach. Two appeared to be White overall and one overall Yellow. They banked over the coastline, accompanied by the deep throbbing roar of their powerful Pratt & Whitney R-2800 engines, as they headed out over Algoa Bay.

Many SAAF machines were delivered directly from the Lockheed factory at Burbank. Fitted with special bomb-bay long-range tanks, they flew to Brazil and then across the Atlantic to Accra from where SAAF pilots flew them to the Union. They were operated by 25 Squadron from the northern boundary of the Port Elizabeth Airfield until early 1943 (see p 40), when they moved to the newly completed St Albans airfield. However, thereafter they were regular callers at Port Elizabeth during their very active patrolling duties.

Notes on the finish

Venturas built in the United States were finished in the standard day-bomber scheme of Dark Green, Dark Earth and Sky using FS-equivalent paints as specified by the British Air Ministry. All machines built prior to July 1942 wore A1 and B roundels with fin flashes which were extended below the tailplane. In SAAF service the undersides were repainted Sky Blue (SAAF 'B' or FS Azure), and included were A-type roundels (not applied to RAF bombers) with Orange in place of the Red. Full fin flashes were applied to all four surfaces. It was quite common for SAAF machines to wear their fuselage roundels further aft than the RAF or US position below the gun turret. The aircraft of 25 Squadron carried large yellow code letters between the serial number and the roundel. A special finish was worn by at least two 25 Squadron aircraft. One of these (No 6037) was finished in White – actually a very pale Blue-Grey – with the upper fuselage decking and flying surfaces in Dark Green and Dark Earth. The code letter, a Yellow J, was outlined with Black to contrast against the 'white'. Fin flashes 24 x 27 in (610 x 686 mm) in size were worn on the outer surfaces only. An overall Yellow Ventura could possibly have been a target tug.

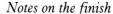

With early morning dew still visible on its fabric surfaces, a Supermarine Walrus circles over Cape Recife on its way to Cape Town sometime in 1943.

Supermarine Walrus

A hoarse crackle with an overtone which sounded like a giant circular saw moving slowly across the sky heralded the arrival of a Supermarine Walrus over the Port Elizabeth Airfield, the apparently slow speed of the 'Shagbag' creating the impression that it was hanging in the air. Mainly during 1942-1943 these aircraft were a common sight at Port Elizabeth, because the city was roughly halfway between the SAAF station at Stamford Hill, Durban (which had temporary accommodation for Fleet Air Arm aircraft, as well as a Fleet Requirements Unit), and Wingfield near Cape Town (which was becoming a ma-

jor FAA facility with accommodation for more than 220 aircraft).

Designed by R. J. Mitchell, of Spitfire fame, the Walrus amphibian, which evolved from the Supermarine Seal of 1921, had an all-metal hull which supported a pair of fabric-covered wings. It was powered by a 775 hp (580 kW) Bristol Pegasus II engine driving a four-bladed pusher propeller. Operating successfully with the FAA in all parts of the world during World War II, the Walrus was regularly seen in South African waters, mainly aboard County class cruisers, including HMS *Dorsetshire* on her last voyage (see p 25).

Notes on the finish
All Walruses seen in South Africa were finished in accordance with the Temperate Sea scheme of Extra Dark Sea Grey and Dark Slate Grey with Sky undersides. Walrus W2714 had the prescribed application of shadow shading as applied to biplanes, which in this case was Dark Sea Grey and Light Slate Grey on the upper surfaces of the lower wing. The non-specular finish had been affected by ultra-violet light and all the colours had faded, which resulted in an evenness of tonal values. An area of Light Slate Grey was applied to the fuselage under the wings. AI and B roundels, fin flashes and rear fuselage serial numbers were displayed. There were no underside roundels.

Short S28 'C' Class Empire Flying Boat

For a period during the war large four-engined Short S28 'C' Class Empire Flying Boats regularly called at Durban. Accompanied by the roar of their four Bristol Pegasus engines, the large silver machines were impressive, especially when gracefully landing on the calm waters of Durban Bay.

In 1935 Imperial Airways took a bold decision and placed an order for twenty flying boats although these had not yet even been designed, and no aircraft of that size had been built in Britain before. Of an all-metal construction with rivetted Alclad skinning on the wings and a semi-monocoque fuselage, they were well-proportioned. In July 1936 'Canopus', the first, undertook its maiden flight, which was a complete success. By 1937 the 'C' class aircraft were in service and in May 1940 'Cleopatra', the last example built, was delivered to its owners.

During the war British Overseas Airways Corporation, the successor to Imperial Airways, used these 200 mph (320 km/h) flying boats as transports on their routes, including the one down Africa to Durban.

Notes on the finish

When the Short S28 'Cleopatra' (G-AFRA) visited Durban during 1942, it wore standard Silver overall finish, apart from its planing hull, which was a dark dirty grey. The BOAC Red, White and Blue wartime flag trim and large registration letters appeared festive at a time when aircraft were drab. The aircraft's name and airline speedbird were prominently displayed below the cockpit.

The early morning light reflects off the calm, silky water of Durban Bay as a Short 'C' Class Empire Flying Boat ('Cleopatra') is towed by a tender.

Lockheed 18 Lodestar

Finished in a hybrid SAA/SAAF scheme, a Lockheed Lodestar on a landing approach is shown with its Fowler flaps fully extended.

In 1940 South African Airways ordered 28 Lockheed 18-08 Lodestars, but on delivery these were taken over by the SAAF as transports. Another machine, with Wright Cyclone engines, was evidently purchased for the South African Red Cross. On 2 February 1945 SAA reintroduced their internal service on a much reduced scale, and at that time a Lodestar flew to Port Elizabeth from Germiston via Bloemfontein every Thursday. With a highly polished finish and blue trim, the aircraft contrasted with the hundreds of camouflaged warplanes at the Port Elizabeth Airfield. One of these examples (ZS-ASY) had been SAAF No 240 during the war. During the 1950s Lodestars were replaced by Vickers Vikings and Douglas DC-3s and DC-4s.

Just as the Lockheed 14 civilian airliner was developed into the Lockheed Hudson to fulfill a British specification, its successor, the Lockheed 18 Lodestar, spawned the B-34 Ventura – also to an RAF requirement. Although the flying surfaces of the Lockheed 14 and 18 were similar, the latter had a smaller and less porcine fuselage and 1 050 hp (785 kW) Pratt & Whitney R-1830 engines instead of the Ventura's brutal R-2800s, and was a more docile aircraft. When taking off, the Lodestar did not develop the deep-throated rumble of the bomber, but sounded more excited and animated as the long, drawn-out whine of its engines moderated to a soft purr on becoming airborne. With a maximum speed of 253 mph (407 km/h) and range of 1 600 miles (2 575 km) with fourteen passengers and a crew of three on board, they performed well.

Notes on the finish

When originally delivered to SAA, the fleet sported highly polished skinning, Black-outlined Cerulean Blue trim and stylized bilingual SAA lettering above the windows, but this was hurriedly altered for SAAF service. The civil registration was replaced by a serial number, while A, A1 and B roundels and full fin flashes were applied. Generally their service scheme was Dark Green, Dark Earth and Sky Blue (SAAF 'B'), but Middle Stone replaced the Dark Green on a number of aircraft used in North Africa.

North American Harvard II

During the first half of 1943 an attractive, beautifully polished, comparatively fast aircraft appeared over the Port Elizabeth Airfield. With its rasping, guttural, throbbing drone the Harvard, one of the greatest trainers of all time, had arrived at 42 Air School. For the following 32 years it would be one of the most common and popular types based at Port Elizabeth.

Operated in large numbers, the Harvard, apart from its major use in the US Air Force, was the backbone of training in the Dominions and continued as such well into the post-war years. Apart from 42 AS, Harvards served with 11 Operational Training Unit, stationed at St Albans. In all nearly 750 of these reliable machines were to fly with the SAAF.

Built as the North American 66 or AT-6, the first SAAF Harvard in full-scale service (the Mk IIa) replaced the Miles Master II as the standard advanced trainer. It differed from the Harvard I in that the fabric-covered fuselage was replaced by an all-metal semi-monocoque structure, the rudder trailing edge straightened and raked and the wingtips squared off.

The Harvard IIa, originally built with a plywood-covered rear fuselage to conserve strategic materials, reverted to the all-metal Mk II standard. By retaining the Mk I welded steel tubular frame of the cockpit section, and fitting easily removed alloy panels, ease of maintenance was greatly improved. Powered by a 600 hp (450 kW) Pratt & Whitney R-1430, a speed of 205 mph (330 km/h), a range of 750 miles (1 207 km) and a ceiling of 23 000 ft (7 010 m) were achieved.

Notes on the finish

The Harvard II had a polished natural metal finish with a matt Dark Green anti-glare panel (originally FS 34087 but sometimes FS 34092 or matt Black) and A, A1 and B roundels with Orange centres. Standard fin flashes and SAAF serial numbers were applied. One of the first at 42 AS (No 7067) had Yellow wheel covers. No Yellow training bands or large serial numbers were worn at that stage, but they were applied to most Harvards later (see p 95). Their polished surfaces contrasted with the dull Silver post-war machines.

With its highly polished finish reflecting the surrounding landscape, a North American Harvard II is shown during a typical approach near the boundary of the Port Elizabeth Airfield.

Consolidated PBY-5A Catalina

On a dull, wet day in April 1943 the even throb of two Pratt & Whitney Twin Wasps, accompanied by a harmonious ringing tone, heralded the arrival of a new type of aircraft. Out of the murk appeared the broad-hulled, square-winged form of a Consolidated PBY-5A Catalina. After circling the city the amphibian came in low over Victoria Park, and seemed to float over the boundary fence as it came in to land. On the fuselage and wings the Dutch flag was worn as insignia, and when the crew disembarked at 7 Air Depot, they wore Dutch naval uniforms.

With the Japanese occupation of the Dutch East Indies, 321 Squadron of the Netherlands Naval Air Service reformed in Ceylon in July 1942, operating as a unit of 222 Group, RAF. With the U-boat offensive continuing unabated, Catalinas were sent to South Africa to operate with 23 Squadron at Darling and 25 Squadron at St Albans. They also spent time at the Port Elizabeth Airfield, where their Dutch and Indonesian crews added a nautical touch to the base. While operating in the Union, the Catalinas carried out night patrols, leaving the Lockheed Venturas to

Surrounded by a wintry landscape, a Consolidated Catalina of the Netherlands Naval Air Service seems to float over the northern boundary fence of the Port Elizabeth Airfield.

concentrate on day flights. In May 1943 Catalina 'T' Y-84 attacked a U-boat while protecting a convoy off Port Elizabeth.

While taxying, the Catalina's narrow-track undercarriage, pylon-supported wings and boom-like tail unit vibrated and shivered unharmoniously, with aerials whipping in all directions. During the very dry, late summer of 1943-1944 the airfield became very dusty, which created a spectacle when Catalinas took off. With engines sounding their urgent, reverberating, musical throb, the wheels threw up clouds of dust which deflected off the hull like spray. Unlike the flying boat version, the amphibians took on water through the undercarriage ports when operated off the sea. Of an all-metal construction with the rear section of the wings fabric-covered, the PBY-5A was powered by 1 200 hp (900 kW) Pratt & Whitney R-1830 engines and had a top speed of 196 mph (315 km/h) and a range of 3 100 miles (4 989 km). As a long-range patrol aircraft the Catalina was popular with aircrews and performed exceptionally well.

Notes on the finish
All 321 Squadron aircraft seen around Port Elizabeth were in a well-maintained condition and were finished in standard US Navy matt Blue Gray with Light Gray undersides. On the Dutch flag insignia AM matt Red and Blue were used. Each aircraft had its original 'Y' serial number and a code in White on the fin. Aircraft 'S' did not display its serial number.

A Catalina on the apron at the St Albans Air Base prior to a patrol. The 'Lady's Slipper' mountain is in the background.

Miles Master II

Banking steeply over St George's Park during the opening ceremony of the Liberty Cavalcade in July 1943, a Miles Master II prepares to give an aerobatics display.

In July 1943 the Liberty Cavalcade, held in St George's Park, was officially opened by Gen Jan Smuts. This was an impressive fund-raising fair at which each of the Allied countries had a stand. The South African Defence Force, for example, displayed a Messerschmitt Bf 109 that had force-landed during the Battle of Britain. (This aircraft is now on display at the South African War Museum, but has been badly repainted.)

Thousands of spectators at the opening parade on the Crusader Ground were surprised by the harsh roar of an overall Yellow Miles Master II pulling out of a steep dive, which proved to be the prelude to one of the most exciting aerobatic displays seen over the city: in fact the Master seemed to be in view throughout the performance.

During 1941 Miles Master IIs were sent to

South Africa as standard advanced trainer to serve with 24 Group of the Joint Air Training Scheme, and more than 400 machines were delivered. The type was agile and somewhat more powerful and dashing than the Harvard, but was generally tricky to fly and difficult to maintain. In addition the type presented the old problem of deteriorating timber structures in semi-tropical climates, and this was to tarnish the reputation of this promising aircraft. As more Harvards became available they replaced the Masters, which were retired by 1943. A few remained in use, however, (some with 11 Operational Training Unit), performing odd tasks until 1945. Sadly, a few of the remaining machines were broken up at 7 Air Depot, and there are none in existence at present.

Developed by the firm of Phillips & Powis from the Miles Kestrel, the Miles Master I, fitted with a 715 hp (535 kW) Rolls-Royce Kestrel engine, was accepted as the RAF's new advanced trainer to replace the Hawker Hart, and 900 were built. Because of a possible shortage of Kestrels, the Mk II was fitted with the 870 hp (650 kW) Bristol Mercury XX, and was also built in large numbers. The aircraft was of an all-wood construction, and the plywood-covered wings of comparatively thick section had an inverted gull form and were attractively faired into the stressed plywood-skinned, semi-monocoque fuselage. Although many of the original machines had the Mk I-type rounded wing-tips, most of those seen in Port Elizabeth had clipped wings. By far the fastest mark, the Master II achieved 260 mph (418 km/h) and had a climb rate of 2 000 ft/min (610 m/min).

Notes on the finish
When delivered from Britain, Miles Masters were finished in the standard RAF Dark Green, Dark Earth and Yellow trainer scheme, with a wavy line separating the upper and lower surfaces. A, A1 and B roundels with 24 x 27 in (610 x 686 mm) fin flashes were worn, but many aircraft wore D-type roundels. Most aircraft were repainted Yellow overall as required in South Africa. Apart from the application of SAAF serial numbers, many aircraft displayed school numbers.

Fairey Battle (Target Tug)

If, as sometimes happened, one heard the smooth drone of a Rolls-Royce Merlin engine and shortly thereafter a flapping flutter, it would inevitably turn out to be a Fairey Battle target tug with a red banner target in tow. By late 1943 Fairey Battles were no longer employed on bomber training duties, but many were transferred to 7 Air Depot, where they were parked while serving as target tugs.

During November 1943, while such a Battle TT flew over Algoa Bay with its banner target towed close in, it passed over the Swedish mercy ship *Gripsholm*. On board were hundreds of United States, Canadian and Latin American citizens released by the Japanese, and they were entering their first port of call after their exchange from Japan.

On the ground the Battles often appeared very clumsy, due to the minimal dihedral and thick section of the wings, one of which very often stood higher than the other due to undercarriage variations.

Notes on the finish
The top surfaces of Battle TTs were finished in Dark Green and Dark Earth and the undersides in the standard Black and Yellow target tug finish.

Above: *The emblem of 7 Air Depot.*

Below: *A Fairey Battle target tug with a banner target flies over the Swedish mercy ship* Gripsholm *in Algoa Bay.*

Showing its beautiful lines to good advantage, a de Havilland Dragon Rapide flies through a dusty thunderstorm near Bloemfontein.

De Havilland 89 Dragon Rapide

In 1941 18 de Havilland 89B Dominie radio training aircraft were supplied to the SAAF, and when these occasionally called at the Port Elizabeth Airfield, they announced their presence by the attractive throaty rumble of their twin 200 hp (150 kW) de Havilland Gipsy Six engines. In addition three private DH 89 Dragon Rapides were impressed into SAAF service, for this type was well-suited to general communications duties. One of these

(ZS-AME) became No 1402 and served with 61 Squadron.

A development of the DH 84 Dragon, and with a family likeness to the four-engined DH 86, the Dragon Rapide was also referred to as the Dragon Six. The knife-like wings and typical DH tail surfaces were of mixed timber and metal construction with a fabric covering, while the timber box fuselage had stringers with fabric covering. The attractive

Rapide had a speed of 157 mph (253 km/h) and a range of 556 miles (895 km).

Notes on the finish
The SAAF Dominies (Nos 1353-1369) were delivered in the standard RAF trainer scheme of Dark Green and Dark Earth with Yellow undersides with A, A1 and B roundels. The A1 roundels were almost equal to the fuselage height. No 1402 was Silver overall with Azure trim, and had A-type roundels on the fuselage and lower wings and the B type on the upper surfaces. The fin flash was stylised.

Consolidated PBY-5 Catalina

Consolidated Catalinas equipped 24 RAF squadrons during World War II. One of these, 262 Squadron, was formed in Britain in September 1942 for service in East Africa. When the squadron's Catalina IBs arrived early in 1943, they were based at Congella, Durban, and also operated from St Lucia and Langebaan, with convoy protection patrols as their main task.

After a large influx of South African personnel, 262 Squadron was transferred to the SAAF as the new 35 Squadron. Although unable to land at Port Elizabeth, the Catalina flying boats were regularly seen over Algoa Bay during their coastal patrols. By July 1945, however, the 'Cats' were replaced by fifteen Short Sunderland Vs, intended for operations in the Far East.

Notes on the finish

A few machines were finished in the 1940-1941 Temperate Sea scheme of Extra Dark Sea Grey and Dark Slate Grey with Sky undersides. They had B and C1 roundels, 24 x 24 in (610 x 610 mm) fin flashes and a White code letter on the fin.

The later maritime scheme (AMO A 664 1942/43), which prescribed White undersides and Extra Dark Sea Grey top surfaces for Sunderlands, was also adopted by Catalinas, but the Temperate Sea scheme was retained for their top surfaces. This finish appeared on a number of 35 Squadron's Catalinas. In the case of one of these (FP288, which was seen over Port Elizabeth), the code letter (G) was in Black. In contrast to the White undersides, which had become stained, its lower hull, which was finished in protective Zinc Chromate, had been marked by harbour oil and dirt. The White, which tended to be too bright for the aircrew, was overpainted – mainly around the motor nacelles and cockpit. In the case of this example a coat of dark Blue Grey had been applied to those areas at a later stage.

A Consolidated Catalina flies over HMS Illustrious *near Durban. The aircraft carrier spent more than two months in that port undergoing a refit.*

Airspeed Oxford II

Right: *An Airspeed Oxford of 61 Squadron flies low over the Swartkops River as the front edge of a cold front moves in from the west.*

Opposite: *An Oxford of 42 Air School formates with another (No 3377), which was reported to have been used by the Officer Commanding 11 Operational Training Unit. The two machines are highlighted by a late afternoon sun and contrast against the background of a bush fire near the Port Elizabeth Airfield in 1944.*

Below: *Parked on the far west side of 42 Air School early in 1945, an Oxford in blind approach markings holds company with an Avro Anson of 61 Squadron.*

By mid-1944 it was noticeable that the number of Airspeed Oxfords operating with 42 Air School had been reduced, while the number of Avro Ansons was on the increase.

Notes on the finish

By this time Oxford colour schemes had undergone various changes – some unique to the SAAF. The RAF Temperate Land upper surface finish worn by most machines sent to South Africa was unnecessary – in fact it was found to be a handicap should an aircraft come down in the veld. An overall Yellow finish was adopted, combined with large fuselage serial numbers, and in many cases the fuselage roundels were omitted. When they were applied, they were positioned further aft, just ahead of the tailplane. Engine cowlings often had trim colours – usually Red or Blue.

To counter the relentless heat of the sun and its effects on wooden aircraft, Silver was introduced as the standard upper surface finish for Oxfords and Ansons. While they retained their Yellow undersides and rudders, Dark Green anti-glare inner nacelle panels were found necessary. A and B roundels and fin flashes were applied, using Blue (SAAF 'BB'), while the large fuselage serial numbers were retained. Of all the aircraft sent to the Port Elizabeth Airfield for disposal after the war, two Oxfords were finished in their original RAF Temperate Land scheme.

A rare Oxford (No 3733) operated by 61 Communications Squadron was Silver overall, with A and B roundels. The unit's standard trim of Azure cowlings and cheat stripe were applied. No serial numbers were worn on the undersides.

Oxfords flown on blind approach exercises wore, in additional to their Silver and Yellow scheme, three Dark Green diagonal fuselage stripes, Green engine nacelles and equilateral triangles of the same colour, but with Yellow centres, outboard of the nacelles. None of these stripes were applied to the undersides.

A Vought Kingfisher of the Fleet Air Arm circles over the coastal village of Schoenmakerskop in January 1944 against the background of thick smoke from a bushfire south of the Port Elizabeth Airfield.

Vought OS2U Kingfisher

In January 1944 a large bushfire broke out south of the Port Elizabeth Airfield and the awe-inspiring sight of massive clouds of smoke slowly moving across the sky, becoming bright orange at night, afforded a fascinating background to the flying activities. After four days the inferno was brought under control and then burnt itself out.

During one of those afternoons an unusual aircraft circled the field, and as it came in to land, the ungainly undercarriage looked as though it had been removed from a cart and stuck onto the fuselage. It was a Vought OS2U Kingfisher two-seater reconnaissance aircraft which, although designed as a float-plane for catapult launching, operated with the Fleet Air Arm over South Africa in a land-plane configuration.

Formed at Durban during July 1943, 726 Squadron (FAA) used two Kingfishers for radar calibration, target towing and communications purposes. The unit had a mixed bag of interesting aircraft, such as a Bristol Beaufighter II and Fairey Swordfish, which were occasionally seen at the Port Elizabeth Airfield en route to Wingfield.

After V-J day, when the FAA payed off most of its aircraft not returned to the United Kingdom or the United States, the two Kingfishers ended up as scrap at Cape Town. The SAAF Museum has a small section of the cockpit area of one of these after it was discovered in a scrap-metal dump in the Cape. The Kingfisher continued the Vought company's interest in fleet reconnaissance aircraft, and bore a strong resemblance to the Corsair, its dashing stablemate. Powered by a 450 hp (335 kW) Pratt & Whitney Wasp Junior, the OS2U 03 had a semi-monocoque fuselage which made use of spot-welding, while the wing was of an all-metal construction with fabric covering aft of the secondary spar, very much like the Corsair.

Notes on the finish
The Kingfisher was finished in standard US Navy Blue Gray for the top surfaces and Light Gray below. B and C1 roundels and standard fin flashes were worn. The words 'Royal Navy' and the serial number were in Black.

Northrop A-17A Nomad

When 'B' Flight of 42 Air School was disbanded in 1944, the unit's Northrop A-17A Nomads were grounded. It was decided to use one of these for fund-raising purposes, and it was therefore taken to the Donkin Reserve aboard a large transporter and parked next to the lighthouse. The public was then given the opportunity to buy special sixpenny stamps, with the objective of covering the aeroplane with these.

As part of a war-time fund-raising effort, a Northrop Nomad is being positioned on the Donkin Reserve. The well-known lighthouse and pyramid are in the background.

R BELLING
© 87

Miles Magister

Banking sharply over Algoa Bay, a Miles Magister reflects the late afternoon sun. Below, the troopship Mauretania prepares to enter the port.

Miles Magister ZS-AMV, which was imported privately before the war, was impressed into the SAAF as No 1448 and served with 42 Air School. Like many service Magisters its spats were removed.

The Magister, the first monoplane trainer to serve with the RAF, was of an all-timber construction with 3-ply wood and fabric covering, and powered by a 130 hp (97 kW) de Havilland Gipsy Major I engine. With a maximum speed of 138 mph (222 km/h) and a climb rate of 850 ft/min (260 m/min), its performance was better than that of the de Havilland Tiger Moth – in fact, it was the same as that of the post-war de Havilland Chipmunk.

However, considerably fewer Magisters than Tiger Moths were built.

Notes on the finish
The Magister was painted Silver overall and wore A-type roundels but no fin flashes. The 42 AS crest was painted on the Black cowling on the nose immediately aft of the spinner.

BELLING © 85

Lockheed PV-1 Ventura

During early 1944 Lockheed PV-1 Venturas made their appearance over Port Elizabeth. Although they emitted the same characteristic deep-throated rumble as the Lockheed B-34, they differed from this variant in that their solid noses looked sleeker, large long-range tanks could be carried outboard of the engines, and they were finished in a new colour scheme.

The PV-1 entered RAF service as the Ventura GR V. More than 140 were delivered to the SAAF and 25 Squadron re-equipped with them and flew in the Port Elizabeth area until May 1944, when they re-equipped with B-34s and left for the Mediterranean Theatre. There-after PV-1s from numerous squadrons were regularly based at Driftsands.

Developed from the B-34, the Lockheed Vega PV-1 was built specifically for US Navy maritime patrol duties. For this purposes it was equipped with ASD-I radar in a solid nose and had an increased internal fuel capacity which extended its range to 1 660 miles (2 672 km). The RAF Boulton-Paul turret gave way to the cleaner Martin 250 CE-13 fitting with a gyro-computing gunsight.

Notes on the finish

An interesting aspect of the finish of the PV-1 Venturas was that they were delivered to the RAF and SAAF in the standard three-colour US Navy scheme. Fuselage decking and flying surfaces were Sea Blue, the flanks Intermediate Blue and the undersides White. The White usually became dirty and discoloured and this colour was sometimes referred to as a pale grey – not to be mistaken for the Light Gray applied to early PV-1s, which were also finished with Blue Gray top surfaces. The US insignia, overpainted with an approximate background colour, were replaced by B and C1 roundels and standard fin flashes, in which Orange replaced the RAF Red, as usual.

Contrasted against a dark, stormy sky, a Fairey Swordfish flies low over Cape Recife, with the lighthouse in the background.

Fairey Swordfish II

During mid-1944 a comparatively large, slow, graceful biplane flew along the Algoa Bay shoreline. The predominantly White Fairey Swordfish II, fitted with rocket rails, displayed South East Asia Command roundels.

Only after the end of 1943 could the Royal Navy afford to send an aircraft carrier into the Indian Ocean, where U-boats were taking their toll. HMS *Battler*, a US-built escort carrier converted from a merchant ship hull, sailed down the East African coast from the Mediterranean. Only 500 ft (152 m) long, equipped for anti-submarine and convoy escort duties, she had aboard 834 Squadron with 9 Swordfish Is, 4 Swordfish IIs and 6 Supermarine Seafire IIcs.

After a spell at sea, with numerous U-boat sightings and interceptions to her credit, she docked at Durban from March 1944 until June to undergo a refit. Her aircraft disembarked and were based at Isipingo, where they flew with the Curtiss Kittyhawks of 11 Operational Training Unit's 'B' Squadron, which was about to transfer to St Albans. (See pp 72, 73 and 86).

Although the Swordfish was considered obsolescent at the outbreak of World War II, it went on to become a legend, operating in all theatres and outclassing its replacement, the Fairey Albacore. Its entire metal structure was fabric-covered and it was powered by a 750 hp (560 kW) Bristol Pegasus 30 engine, which gave it a maximum speed of 139 mph (224 km/h), a ceiling of 10 700 ft (3 261 m) and a range of 1 030 miles (1 658 km). The Swordfish II had strengthened lower wings to enable it to carry eight 60-lb rockets.

Notes on the finish

Although the 1943-1944 standards for Fleet Air Arm carrier aircraft specified the Temperate Sea scheme, coastal patrol colours of White undersides and fuselage flanks were introduced for rocket-carrying Swordfish IIs. The contemporary small SEAC roundels were worn, with only a blue rectangle for the fin flashes, and an aircraft code letter in Dark Slate Grey ahead of the words 'Royal Navy' and the serial number in Black. At least two of 834 Squadron's Swordfish Is wore a Temperate Sea scheme which was modified for some unknown reason. The disruptive pattern on the top surfaces of their wings and tailplanes was exaggerated by introducing what looked like Medium Sea Grey but which did not conform to the standard pattern. This could have been for night operations.

Blackburn Roc

Once the Fleet Air Arm had adopted Wingfield as a major base, a variety of interesting support machines were seen there. One of these was the Blackburn Roc, a pre-war fighter design based on the Blackburn Skua fleet dive bomber to which a power-operated four-gun turret was added. As the naval counterpart of the Boulton-Paul Defiant, the Roc suffered from the same shortcomings as the Defiant, and Rocs and Skuas were thus relegated to target tug and training duties. One Roc and two Skuas based at Wingfield operated with 789 Fleet Requirements Squadron.

Fitted with a 900 hp (675 kW) Bristol Perseus XII engine, the Roc achieved a maximum speed of no more than 200 mph (322 km/h), a climb rate of 1 130 ft/min (344 m/min) to a service ceiling of 14 600 ft (4 450 m), and could not cope with contemporary fighters. For target-towing duties the gun turret was removed.

Notes on the finish
Although the official FAA finish requirement for target tugs was the Temperate Sea scheme with undersides striped in Black and Yellow, L3127 had an overall Yellow finish with Black diagonal stripes. However, these did not conform to the standard spacing, but instead related to the insignia and cockpit positions. The B, C and C1 roundels had faded badly and the non-standard White serial number on a Yellow field contrasted with the Black.

A Blackburn Roc target tug flies over the West Coast just north of Cape Town.

Curtiss P-40N Kittyhawk IV

One of the first Curtiss P-40N Kittyhawks to operate with 'B' Squadron of 11 Operational Training Unit on its transfer to St Albans from Isipingo arrived over the Port Elizabeth Airfield in mid-1944, and the smooth, powerful drone of its Allison engine reverberated over the airfield as the aircraft performed a series of impressive rolls. Coming round over South End with its undercarriage down, the engine idling except for occasional bursts of power, the clean, desert-camouflaged fighter then carried out a perfect landing and taxied into 7 Air Depot.

Thereafter the Kittyhawks, North American Harvards and Miles Masters of 11 OTU were regular callers at the Port Elizabeth Airfield, where they underwent maintenance overhauls at 7 Air Depot, followed by test flights (which were carried out over the airfield), before returning to base at St Albans.

Testing the Kittyhawks usually involved an interesting procedure. Before taxying out to the field, the pilot would gun the engine while parked on the apron, with four or five ground crew draped over the tailplane as human ballast. As the revolutions built up the smooth Allison sound became a droning roar with an attractive bell-like tone and while the airframe quivered, the slipstream wrapped the khaki-clad forms around the tailplane. Test flights were exciting, as the aircraft being put through its paces was taken through very fast rolls over the full length of the airfield.

Although not able to compete with the Supermarine Spitfire or Messerschmitt Bf 109F

Right: *Early in 1944 one of the first Curtiss Kittyhawks to arrive in Port Elizabeth approaches the Port Elizabeth Airfield over South End, the old, dilapidated, colourful quarter since demolished and replaced by some of the most monotonous architecture to be found in the city.*

Opposite above: *Still in a United States camouflage scheme, a Kittyhawk undergoes an engine run-up at 7 Air Depot prior to a test flight. Note the clean A, the thick White stripe of the fin flash and the oxidation, which has obscured the serial number.*

Opposite below: *Showing to advantage the characteristic 90-degree turn of the Kittyhawk's undercarriage on retraction, a P-40 from 'A' Squadron of 11 Operational Training Unit takes off from Waterkloof in 1944.*

as an all-altitude fighter in the Desert Campaign, the Kittyhawk proved to be a sturdy machine, ideal for ground attack, and was used as such by the SAAF in North Africa and Italy. Many of these machines were later allocated the role of operational trainers in the Union of South Africa.

Developed from the Curtiss P-36 Mohawk by way of the P-40A, B and C Tomahawk, the final service version (P-40N Kittyhawk IV) was possibly the most attractive. With a 1 350 hp (1 000 kW) Allison V-1710 engine, the Kittyhawk had a speed in excess of 350 mph (563 km/h), a service ceiling of 30 000 ft (9 144 m) and a range of 810 miles (1 305 km) or 1 190 (1 915 km) with a long-range tank.

Notes on the finish

Most of the initial 11 OTU Kittyhawks at St Albans were finished in Dark Earth, Middle Stone and Azure (FS 35231). Usually in good condition, they had a thin Yellow fuselage stripe with a White identification letter forward of the C1 roundel. B and C wing roundels and fin flashes were standard. Later aircraft joining the unit were finished mainly in Dark Green, Dark Earth and BS Azure, with broad Yellow fuselage and wing bands over which the serial number was painted on the underside. Spinners were painted Dark Green and Dark Earth, or with concentric bands of Blue, White and Orange. At least two machines were seen in their original US Olive Drab (FS 34087) with a Medium Green (FS 34092) outline pattern, and Neutral Gray (FS 36118). One retained its upper wing US star insignia, and the other had a Yellow band around the fuselage only (see right above). The shark's mouth, synonymous with Kittyhawks, was painted on No 5082 (16) of 'A' Squadron. This magnificent example was painted in the usual desert finish with a White spinner and wingtips and wore B and C1 roundels, while those on the underside were hybrids – the Blue was of the C dimension, but the Orange diameter conformed to A standards. In this case the individual aircraft number rather than the serial number was painted on the underside Yellow bands as well as on a Yellow rectangle ahead of the fuselage roundel.

Flying over Cookhouse in the Eastern Cape, a Supermarine Spitfire F VIII in a special finish heads towards East London.

Supermarine Spitfire F VIII

When in mid-1944 the first Supermarine Spitfire to visit the Eastern Cape arrived at East London, it seemed unexpectedly different. The beautiful elliptical wings were too pointed, it wasn't camouflaged, but finished in an overall blue, and the fuselage shape was broken by a long-range slipper tank. The reason was that this example (JF294) was an RAF Spitfire F VIII with pointed high-altitude long-span wings. Having flown from Cairo to the Cape a few months earlier, it still wore its special finish.

After touring the Union, JF294 returned to Waterkloof, where the blue finish was removed. Now in a natural metal finish, it became SAAF No 5501, the personal aircraft of Col D. H. Loftus, Officer Commanding 11 Operational Training Unit. Presently this example is housed in the South African National Museum of Military History, and appears somewhat theatrical, with a polished mirror-like finish. Perhaps this special Spitfire will one day be restored to its true wartime appearance.

To counter the high-altitude intruder Junkers Ju 86Ps flying over Britain at will, a special high-altitude fighter version of the Spitfire, the Mk VII, was built. With pointed long-span wings, a pressurized cockpit and a Rolls-Royce Merlin 71 engine, a ceiling of 44 000 ft (13 411 m) was possible. Its successor, the Mk VIII, was built in fighter (F), high-altitude fighter (HF) and low-altitude fighter (LF) versions fitted with a retractable tail-wheel, short-span ailerons and cleanshaped Aero-Vee tropical filter in place of the heavy Vokes type previously used on desert Spitfire Vs, and served in large numbers in the Far East, amongst other services with the Royal Australian Air Force.

It is believed that JF294 served in Italy. As it was an early production model, it had the original elliptical rudder. Although it had HF wings, it must be referred to as an F VIII, for it was fitted with a 1 520 hp (1 140 kW) Merlin 61 engine. It was, at that time, one of the best performers in the skies of South Africa, with a maximum speed of 404 mph (650 km/h), a ceiling of 43 000 ft (13 106 m), a rate of climb of 6,5 mins to 20 000 ft (6 000 m) and a range of 660 miles (1 062 km), or 1 180 miles (1 899 km) with a long-range tank.

Notes on the finish
Prior to regulation AP 2656A of October 1944, which defined high-altitude fighter colours (Medium Sea Grey upper surfaces and Photo Reconnaissance Unit Blue below), a generalized specification existed, dated December 1942. More than likely the overall PRU Blue finish of JF294 was determined by the latter. On its arrival in South Africa an oxidation mark swept back along most of the fuselage length, and this was enhanced by some flowing oil leaks. RAF B roundels were worn on the fuselage and upper surfaces, as well as Red and Blue fin flashes. After the removal of the RAF paint scheme the aircraft wore A-type roundels of a non-standard size, and those on the wing upper surfaces were unusually far inboard. The present B, C and C1 roundels and fin flashes, and the presentation of the underwing serial number, appear authentic, and must have officially replaced the A-type roundels for display in the museum.

Supermarine Seafire IIc

On 21 March 1944 834 Squadron arrived at Stamford Hill, having disembarked from HMS *Battler* while she underwent a refit in Durban. The fighter component of the unit, equipped with six Seafire IIcs, moved to Isipingo where the Curtiss Kittyhawks of 11 Operational Training Unit were based. When 834 Squadron re-embarked on *Battler*, the Seafires were replaced by Grumman Wildcats, which were more suitable for operating from the small escort carriers.

Developed from the Spitfire Vb, the Seafire Ib was virtually a Spitfire with an arrester hook. The next version (the IIc) was designed with a Spitfire Vc wing and had a reinforced airframe for catapult launching. Powered by a 1 340 hp (1 000 kW) Rolls-Royce Merlin 45 or 46, which gave it a top speed of 333 mph (536 km/h), a ceiling of 32 000 ft (9 754 m) and a normal range of 500 miles (805 km), the IIc had its limitations as a fleet fighter.

Notes on the finish
Although the Temperate Sea scheme was specified for all Fleet Air Arm fighters, many Seafires were initially delivered in the RAF fighter scheme of BS Dark Green, Ocean Grey and Medium Sea Grey. The illustrated example (LR702 from 834 Squadron), which was based at Isipingo for a spell, had such a scheme with small South East Asia Command roundels on all surfaces, and including fin flashes of two-thirds Blue and one-third White. On the port side, behind the cockpit, there was quite a large area of Dark Green overpainted in Ocean Grey on which the code letter Z outlined in White had been applied. This was repeated in Black on the underside of the nose, behind the spinner. In the case of many Seafire IIs the undersides of their nose cowlings were finished in BS Sky Blue.

A Supermarine Seafire flies over HMS Battler, *at speed near Durban.*

North American Harvard (Target Tug)

When 11 Operational Training Unit was established at St Albans and later at the Port Elizabeth Airfield, their Harvards were also regularly seen flying around Port Elizabeth. When 'B' flight was disbanded, a few Harvards took over target-towing duties on a reduced scale from this flight's Northrop Nomads, and in early 1945 Nos 7140 and 7128 were regularly seen in this capacity. On 11 May 1945 No 7128 flew very low over the Central Hill area of Port Elizabeth to drop leaflets for a fund-raising campaign.

Notes on the finish

Harvard TTs were finished in Yellow overall, with Black diagonal stripes on the upper and lower surfaces, as was the case with No 7140. B and C roundels were applied, but apart from the stripes, there were no markings on the undersides. Possibly due to being repainted, No 7128 was Yellow overall, with Black diagonal stripes on the wings and stabilizer undersides only.

Above: *A North American Harvard target tug in a shallow dive over Cape Recife, with the Port Elizabeth Airfield and city in the background.*

Right: *Flying low over the Port Elizabeth Central Hill area in May 1945, a Harvard target tug is shown dropping leaflets.*

A Grumman Hellcat flies low over St Croix, an island in Algoa Bay.

Grumman F6F-5 Hellcat F II

Late in 1944 the first of a powerful new breed of US Navy fighters made its appearance over Port Elizabeth. Its characteristic square-cut wings, large tailplane and bulky fuselage signalled it as a Grumman F6F-5 Hellcat as the Fleet Air Arm machine banked steeply over Walmer. A few days later another was seen flying low over Algoa Bay while the deep rumble of its powerful engine reverberated over the water.

Somewhat larger and more powerful than the Grumman F4F Wildcat, the Hellcat was designed to replace the former at a time when Grumman could incorporate, to advantage, the experience gained by aircrews flying against the Japanese. Powered by a Pratt & Whitney R-2800 engine, it attained a maximum speed of 371 mph (597 km/h), an initial climb rate of 3 410 ft/min (1 039 m/min) and a range of 1 040 miles (1 674 km) or 1 530 miles (2 462 km) with a long-range tank. The Hellcat was more than a match for most Japanese fighters, and during the closing stages of the Pacific War it and the Vought Corsair reigned supreme as fleet fighters.

Most of the aircraft attached to 896 Squadron were of the FB II type, which was equipped with rocket rails below the wings.

Notes on the finish
One of the first Hellcats over Port Elizabeth was JX702. It was finished in the Temperate Sea scheme and had South East Asia Command roundels in six positions. The temporary code 2Q indicates that the machine was more than likely from 896 Squadron, before rocket rails were installed. The first unit to leave the Union for the Far East was 804 Squadron, which used the initial code letters 1A, 1B and so on, and 898 Squadron had at that time not yet been formed. On operations 804 Squadron used the code B6, 896 Squadron the codes B7 and B8 and 898 Squadron the code B9. Hellcat 2Q had a somewhat washed-out finish and the number 702 was painted on the nose in large White numerals.

Vought F4U Corsair

A Vought Corsair 'with everything down' makes its approach to HMS Illustrious *after the ship's refit in Durban. (Note the ship's colours as compared with those on p 63.)*

From August to September 1944 HMS *Illustrious* underwent a refit in Durban (see p 63) and her aircraft (Vought F4U Corsairs from 1830 Squadron and 1833 Squadron, as well as the Fairey Barracudas of 810 Squadron) were based at Wingfield. During their stay the powerful fighters with their inverted gull-wings became well known for their exceptionally low flying over the surrounding suburbs of Cape Town.

The Fleet Air Arm received their first Corsair Is (F4U-1) in 1943, while the Mk II (F4U-1D) version served mainly in the Far East. Their clipped wings were necessary for stowage on Royal Navy aircraft carriers. Operating alongside Hellcats in the US Navy and FAA, these two types gained the nickname 'the terrible twins'. Both aircraft were generally superior to Japanese fighters.

First flown in 1940, the Corsair (at the time the most powerful naval fighter ever built) had inverted gull wings which made it possible to fit a large propeller, shorter undercarriage and easily folded wings. With a 2 000 hp (1 500 kW) Pratt & Whitney R-2800 engine, it had a maximum speed of 417 mph (670 km/h) and a range of 1 015 miles (1 633 km), which was a great improvement over the Wildcat. It was built with an all-metal structure and had wings that were fabric-covered aft of the main spar. The metal skinning was spot-welded.

Notes on the finish

The example shown (6C – JT324) clearly illustrates the contrast in colours when US-built aircraft were finished in approximate FS and BS equivalents. The top surfaces are FS Olive Drab and Sea Grey and the undersides Sky, while the fuselage C1-type roundel was overpainted and replaced by the small South East Asia Command version, and the fin flash Red overpainted White. When HMS *Illustrious* returned to the Far East, the insignia were brought up to the latest standards (see p 99).

Fairey Barracuda

During 1944 HMS *Illustrious* underwent a two-month refit in Durban, and during this time her Fairey Barracuda IIs of 810 Squadron were based at Wingfield. When these heavy, cluttered, interesting aircraft flew low over Table Bay, the steady drone of their Rolls-Royce Merlin engines reverberated over the sea. The characteristic high, braced tailplane was necessary to avoid turbulence from the independent Youngman flaps. After the defeat of Japan most Barracuda squadrons were disbanded, after having been active in the Pacific Campaign as well as in Europe. In 1947 the radar-equipped Barracuda III entered service with the Fleet Air Arm in limited numbers.

Designed as a replacement for the Fairey Albacore, the Barracuda II, powered by a 1 640 hp (1 225 kW) Rolls-Royce Merlin 32 engine, had a speed of 278 mph (447 km/h), a climb rate of 900 ft/min (274 m/min) and a range of 524 miles (843 km) with a bomb load of 2 000 lb (900 kg) or 853 miles (1 373 km) when carrying a torpedo of 1 610 lb (725 kg). This performance dropped considerably in the subtropical Pacific environment.

Notes on the finish
Fairey Barracuda P9961 (2P) of 810 Squadron was finished in the standard Temperate Sea scheme and had large Blue and White South East Asia Command roundels on the fuselage and wing upper surfaces, as well as the usual fin flashes. The squadron code letters were in White.

Flying low over Table Bay towards Cape Town, a Fairey Barracuda from HMS Illustrious *simulates a torpedo dropping run.*

Hawker Hurricane II

By the end of 1944 Curtiss Kittyhawks were being lost at an unacceptable rate, mainly due to minor accidents, and consequently Hawker Hurricanes began operations with 11 Operational Training Unit at St Albans. The first two to call at the Port Elizabeth Airfield were in a comparatively good condition and were fitted with long-range wing tanks.

Right above: *Hawker Hurricanes of 11 Operational Training Unit flying along the Algoa Bay shore. One of the aircraft has a minor mechanical problem and is trailing smoke. Note the Mediterranean Light Blue undersides on this recently overhauled machine.*

Right: *Flying low over the Swartkops River mouth, these Hurricanes are on their way to the gunnery range. The remains of numerous sailing vessels, many wrecked during a gale at the turn of the century, may be found along this stretch of the coast.*

On 15 February 1945 11 OTU transferred from St Albans to the Port Elizabeth Airfield where they operated from the north side of the airfield, which in 1942 had been occupied by 25 Squadron. About 30 Hurricanes lined up on the east side of the old pre-war hangar and about 15 Harvards on the west side. For the following few months flying over Port Elizabeth was dominated by Hurricanes, the droning note of their Rolls-Royce Merlin engines heralding their coming and going throughout the day. The activity at the airfield was like that of a combat unit, with a mobile control tower, bowsers, tent accommodation and armaments. At a gunnery and bombing range established at St Georges Strand north of the Swartkops River mouth, target floats were anchored off-shore for gunnery and bombing practice.

By the end of July 1945, shortly before V-J Day, 11 OTU ceased to operate. A few Hurricanes returned to Waterkloof, but most remained standing on the aprons at 7 Air Depot until disposed of in 1947. Bought by a scrap metal dealing company, they lingered in a storage yard until they disappeared in the early 1950s.

The Hurricane – a real thoroughbred – evolved from the Hawker Fury, and the same type of construction was used, except for the low, all-metal wing designed to accommodate the retractable undercarriage. Powered by a 1 185 hp (885 kW) Rolls-Royce Merlin XX engine, the IIB and IIC had a maximum speed of 330 mph (531 km/h), a climb rate of 2 850 ft/min (869 m/min), a service ceiling of 33 000 ft (10 058 m) and a range of 460 miles (740 km), extended to 970 miles (1 561 km) with long-range tanks. The IIB was fitted with twelve .303 machine guns, which differed from the armament of the IIC (four 20-mm Hispano cannon). While operating with 11 OTU both types were tropicalised, with deep Vokes filters fitted under the nose.

Notes on the finish

While the first two aircraft with a Dark Earth and Middle Stone finish seen at 7 Air Depot had Light Mediterranean Blue undersides, it looked as though they had recently undergone a major overhaul. The majority of the aircraft, however, were well worn, with oil and exhaust stains mixed with dust that sometimes blended with the colour scheme. About a quarter of the aircraft were finished in Dark Earth, Middle Stone and Azure, 60 per cent in Dark Green, Dark Earth and Azure or Sky Blue (SAAF 'B'), and the remainder Brown or Green overall or, in one case, two shades of Green. The spinners were Dark Green, Dark Earth, Black or Yellow.

The B, C and C1 roundels were a mixture of RAF and SAAF types with the correct BS Blue, Red or Orange, while others used the paler SAAF Insignia Blue 'AA'. Yellow operational trainer bands were applied to the wings and fuselage aft of the roundel, and a Yellow rectangle ahead of the insignia. The squadron code letters were applied to the rectangle and the aircraft letter or number to the band in Black. 'A' Squadron based at Waterkloof used the code letters DB and 'B' Squadron at Port Elizabeth the letters GL. These letters corresponded to codes worn by 2 and 5 Squadron in North Africa and Italy.

Hurricane No 5210 (R) (p 80) is a good example of a dirty aircraft – old and repainted on numerous occasions. It sports RAF roundels and a finish of Dark Green, Dark Earth

A Hurricane performing aerobatics over the Swartkops River estuary, with Swartkops village in the far distance. The wave action and currents prevalent at this notoriously dangerous river mouth can be clearly seen.

Parked alongside the rainsoaked north boundary road of the Port Elizabeth Airfield in June 1945 are these Hurricanes of 11 Operational Training Unit.

and Azure Grey/Blue, while No 5218 (II) is a cleaner machine, with SAAF roundels and the same colour scheme on the upper surfaces but SAAF Sky Blue 'B' undersides. Note that where the leading edge paint has worn off ahead of the starboard roundel on No 5210, the original Leading Edge Yellow is visible, as well as BS Sky Blue, not intended for RAF fighters. All the blues on this aircraft seem non-standard. The underside blue with

which it was finished at the time of the painting was not true BS Azure, but Methuen 20 C4. This had been painted over an interesting deep Azure (Methuen 20 C6) which appears to have been applied in North Africa, possibly as a substitute for Light Mediterranean Blue.

Hurricane No 5205 (P) (p 81) is unusual in that the upper surfaces were finished in a variation of Dark Earth with a slight grey cast

(Methuen 6F 3-4) and a variation of Azure (FS 35240). No 5265 (26) (below) was another rare bird, finished in Dark Green and Light Green, with BS Azure undersides. The old RAF roundels contained Blue 'AA' contrasting sharply with the correctly painted insignia on No 5211 (5). No 5285, on display at the South African National Museum of Military History, is unfortunately poorly finished.

Avro Anson

During 1944 Avro Ansons replaced many of the Airspeed Oxfords at 42 Air School.

Notes on the finish

By 1944 the standard scheme for Avro Ansons was Silver upper surfaces and Yellow undersides and rudders. Typical of the minority fitted with a Bristol IV turret and with smooth engine cowlings, No 4518 wore B, C and C1 roundels and Black code letters (right).

Anson No 3268 (AO) (right below) and No 3294 (AH) (p 84) are typical of the Ansons in their last few months of service. All part of the same flight, their BS Light Green antiglare panels were painted on noses painted with different patterns of Red. While No 3294 displayed the correct revised insignia, No 3268 retained the old fin flashes and wore C1 roundels with incorrect proportions. Its window framing had been modified, as was also recorded on a few other Ansons late in the war.

Towards the end of hostilities the Yellow undersides gave way to an overall Silver scheme, and this was seen on a minority of machines. Large fuselage serial numbers were sometimes displayed, and instead of codes, coloured engine cowlings (usually Red, Blue and Black) were used (p 84).

Above: *The emblem of 11 Operational Training Unit.*

Right above: *An Avro Anson fitted with a Bristol turret about to touch down.*

Right: *An Anson banks over the Coega salt pans.*

Apart from the general note on colour variations, there were a few major exceptions. Anson No 4347 (K) (p 85) had pale khaki undersides. No explanation for its use has been found, although it appears to be the standard Yellow, to which Black had mistakenly been added. The Blue in the RAF B, C and CI roundels was SAAF Sky Blue 'AA'.

During June 1945, Anson No 4347, together with a few others, observed one of the many corvettes which underwent sea trials after a refit in Port Elizabeth. After testing all armaments, including depth charges, the all-clear signal was sounded, and this was a signal for local fishing boats to come and collect a good haul of dead or stunned fish.

At least one Anson, No 4530 (see p 64), served with 61 Squadron. It was finished in Silver overall and had the standard Deep Azure trim, nose and nacelles. A and B roundels were applied, but there was no underside serial number. Some of the last serving Ansons in 1947 wore Springbok roundels.

Two Ansons in formation over the St Albans Air Base in April 1945. No 3294 was rebuilt after crashing in 1942.

*An Anson banks over
HMS* Honesty, *which is
undergoing sea trials after a
refit in Port Elizabeth.*

Lockheed PV-1 Ventura

After 25 Squadron left Port Elizabeth, Lockheed PV-1 Venturas from other units were regularly seen over the area. Among these a few early production machines could be identified by their nose windows, which resembled the B-34 type.

Apart from the purely structural differ- ences, the aircraft could also be identified by their Blue Gray and Light Gray finish. The two colours were separated along the fuselage centreline by a soft airbrush line. When seen from below, these aircraft, which were usual- ly fitted with long-range tanks, appeared to be painted Light Gray overall.

Curtiss P-40N Kittyhawk

A lone 11 Operational Training Unit Curtiss P-40 Kittyhawk was often seen flying with the Hawker Hurricanes. This was No 5106, the last airworthy example at the base, and coincidently the last to be taken on charge by the SAAF.

Notes on the finish
Kittyhawk No 5106 was finished in FS Dark Green, Dark Earth and Sky – an unusual underside colour for 11 OTU aircraft. The usual Yellow bands and Black serial numbers were worn, while the spinner was White. It is very likely that this aircraft, then with a Green spinner and with no fuselage band, was disposed of in 1947. The remains of such an aircraft were found on a smallholding near St Albans, and are currently in the care of the SAAF Museum. Another Kittyhawk, with a polished metal overall finish and fitted with a long-range tank (said to be the aircraft of the base Commanding Officer), was occasionally seen at 7 Air Depot. It wore RAF B, C and C1 roundels, and had a matt Dark Green antiglare panel and a Yellow fuselage band which bore a Black letter V.

Above: *A Kittyhawk with an all-metal finish, based at 42 Air School.*

Left: *A Curtiss Kittyhawk beating up the Port Elizabeth Airfield. A number of 11 Operational Training Unit Hurricanes are lined up along the north boundary, and Victoria Park can be seen in the background.*

Lockheed PV-1 Ventura

A Lockheed PV-1 Ventura flies over the Swedish refugee ship Drottningholm *in a Mediterranean setting. The ship was a regular caller at Port Elizabeth during 1945 while transporting German nationals back to Europe. Note the unusual Martin-type intakes above the Ventura's engine nacelles.*

When 17 Squadron, operating in the Mediterranean Theatre, re-equipped with Vickers Warwicks, twenty of the unit's Lockheed PV-1 Venturas were flown to the Union in four flights of five aircraft each during January 1945. One flight was directed to Port Elizabeth, but encountered such bad weather at the coast that one aircraft ground-looped on the Port Elizabeth Airfield and another force-landed near Somerset East. Fortunately the remaining three somehow managed to get down safely.

Notes on the finish

The machine that ground-looped, JS953 (G) (below), was an interesting example. In common with Ventura GR Vs delivered to the RAF it had retained the standard three-tone US Navy scheme while serving with 17 Squadron. However, during the latter half of 1944, when 17 Squadron undertook night shipping reconnaisance and harbour strike duties, Black undersides were introduced. This attractive hybrid scheme can be related to Air Ministry Directive AMO (AL No 8) of October 1944, which prescribed Extra Dark Sea Grey upper surfaces with Black undersides for special coastal duties. Ultra-violet light had affected the upper surfaces: while the non-specular Sea Blue (FS 35042) fuselage decking had faded, the wings, tailplane and nacelles (also in Sea Blue, but conforming to FS 25042) had retained most of their original tone. The washed-out decking had the appearance of a different, paler colour. The Intermediate Blue (FS 35164) had faded slightly, while the hurriedly applied Black undersides peeled off in patches to reveal the original White.

Although a SAAF machine, JS953 retained its original RAF serial number, and the B and C1 roundels had Red. The aircraft code letter was an Orange G, and the wheel covers were Brown.

In early 1945 six additional ex-RAF Venturas were based at the Port Elizabeth Airfield. They had very faded top surfaces that appeared to be more Dark Sea Grey than Sea Blue or Intermediate Blue, and Black undersides. One of these, JT856, wore RAF B and C1 roundels, a Red N forward of the roundel and a matching P aft.

Above: *A Martin 250 CE-13 turret, as fitted to some Venturas.*

Right: *A Ventura banking over Bird Island on the east side of Algoa Bay.*

JT 856

N⊙P

BELLIN © 84

Grumman Avengers thunder across Algoa Bay, with storm clouds building up in the south.

Grumman TBF-1 Avenger

On 23 March 1945 three aircraft with a typical Grumman appearance thundered across Algoa Bay in loose formation. As they neared the airfield, they were identified as Grumman TBF-1 Avenger Is, and when they broke sharply to port their characteristic long outward-retracting undercarriage could be seen. The aircraft were from 851 Squadron, Fleet Air Arm, having disembarked from their escort carrier, HMS *Shah*, which had docked in Durban for a five-week stay. During this period the aircraft were based at Stamford Hill, and three of their number flew to Wingfield, with a stop-over at Port Elizabeth.

The FAA machines, supplied by the United States under lend-lease arrangements, carried out many attacks on the Japanese mainland before the end of World War II. Soon after August 1945, however, most British squadrons disbanded and returned their aircraft to the US or dumped them at sea. By the end of 1946 the Avenger had disappeared from the Royal Navy. In 1953, however, the specialized AS-4 joined the FAA in limited numbers, until replaced by the Fairey Gannet.

Designed as a replacement for the Douglas Devastator, the Grumman TBF-1 Avenger bore a strong family resemblance to the Wildcat and Hellcat. The Avenger entered service in the Pacific during 1942 and operated successfully with the FAA in the European and Pacific theatres as a three-seater carrier-borne torpedo-bomber and antisubmarine strike aircraft.

Powered by a 1 850 hp (1 385 kW) Wright Cyclone GR-2600 engine, the Avenger I had a maximum speed of 260 mph (418 km/h) and a range of more than 1 000 miles (1 609 km) with a bomb load of 2 000 lb (900 kg). Most of the 10 000 in service during World War II were built by General Motors.

Notes on the finish

The Grumman Avengers of 851 Squadron were finished in the Temperate Sea scheme with Sky undersides, but the paintwork showed signs of ultra-violet fading. Original B and CI roundels were overpainted with Extra Dark Sea Grey as a background for small South East Asia Command roundels. The fin flashes had a two-thirds Blue rectangle, with the remaining one-third White. White SEAC bands were applied to all flying surfaces. A two-letter code outlined in White was worn, and the individual aircraft letter was reproduced in White above the fin stripe.

Avro Lancaster I

On Sunday, 8 April 1945, an Avro Lancaster appeared, seemingly not far above the tall pines between the suburb of Walmer and the Port Elizabeth Airfield, and the sound of its Rolls-Royce Merlin engines built up to a roaring crescendo. After having carried out a beat-up of the base, the predominantly black aircraft banked sharply and circled the city twice before heading for St Albans, which had runways that could bear the large bomber's weight, unlike the Port Elizabeth Airfield. On the following day this impressive aeroplane flew over the city centre, affording the public a good view of one of the most successful bombers of the war.

Lancaster PD328 was a standard Mk I bomber with the mid-upper gun turret replaced by an astrodome. Named 'Aries', it was used by the Empire Air Navigation School for long-range excursions. On this particular flight it flew from Britain to North America, North Africa and down Africa to the Union, calling at Pretoria, Cape Town, Port Elizabeth and Durban. The RAF were planning to operate large numbers of Lancasters and later Lincolns against the Japanese, but as it happened, this was not necessary.

A long-span, four-engined version of the not-so-successful Avro Manchester, which was powered by twin Rolls-Royce Vulture engines, the Lancaster was fitted with 1 460 hp (1 090 kW) Rolls-Royce Merlin 20, 22 or 1 640 hp (1 225 kW) Merlin 24 engines. Dimensionally not much larger than the Douglas Dakota or Consolidated Catalina, it carried a bomb load of 14 000 lb (6 300 kg) a distance of 1 660 miles (2 672 km) with a maximum speed of 287 mph (462 km). A specially modified version could carry the staggering 22 000-lb (9 900 kg) Grand Slam bomb 1 040 miles (1 674 km). Generally of conventional construction, the fuselage had a pair of extruded longerons linked by cross-beams to form the backbone from which the bomb load was carried.

There is a fascinating story attached to the birth of this remarkable aircraft. It is said that Roy Chadwick (see p 20), who was never

one to be deterred, ordered one of Avro's hangars cleared and had a Manchester wheeled in. After the machine was stripped to all its components, he called a meeting of selected engineers, technicians and draughtsmen and proceeded to give each one preliminary instructions on how the wingspan would be increased to accommodate four Rolls-Royce Merlin engines. His instruction was to 'make it simple, and try to imagine that six months hence you might have the job of repairing or overhauling this machine'. The result was the Lancaster.

Notes on the finish
In the standard Bomber Command finish consisting of the Temperate Land scheme with Black (Night) undersides, PD328 displayed unique insignia specially devised for it: both C-type upper wing and CI fuselage roundels had late South East Asia Command white rectangles, but the Red centres were retained (below). The serial number was in Red and the name below the cockpit in White.

Avro Lancaster 'Aries' flying low over central Port Elizabeth, with the Donkin Reserve in the foreground.

Bristol Beaufighter II and Grumman F6F Hellcat FB II

On Sunday, 22 April 1945, shortly after 13h00, 21 Grumman F6F Hellcat FB IIs of 896 Squadron, en route to Durban to join their carrier, HMS *Ameer*, arrived over Port Elizabeth. While landing to refuel, a lone attendant Bristol Beaufighter II circled overhead, and the smooth drone of Rolls-Royce Merlin engines contrasted with the deep rumble of Pratt & Whitney R-2800s. Many of the aircraft of 804, 896, 898 and 881 Squadrons (formed at Wingfield for operations in the Pacific) were shipped directly from the United States and modified to Fleet Air Arm standards at Wingfield. After 'working up' the units then joined their ships.

The Beaufighter was from 789 Squadron, one of a number of Fleet Requirements Units which served with the FAA. The type had an interesting background: Bristol originally embarked on the development of a long-range fighter which the RAF urgently required, by utilising the wings and tail assembly of the Beaufort, married with a new fuselage and Bristol Hercules engines. Carrying a powerful armament, the Beaufighter was a formidable machine and proved successful as a night-fighter. Yet later, armed with rockets, cannon and torpedoes, it established itself as an outstanding strike aircraft.

In the Middle and Far East the type also established an enviable record and was referred to by the Japanese as 'Whispering Death'. At least five FAA FRU's were equipped with Beaufighter IIs, and Beaufighter Xs successfully served with the SAAF, amongst others with 16 and 19 Squadron in the Mediterranean Theatre. In South Africa Beaufighters were usually seen along the coast when naval aircraft movements were underway. The remains of one of these aircraft was discovered by the SAAF Museum in a Cape Town scrap metal yard in the mid-1970s.

The Mk II, fitted with two 1 260 hp (940 kW) Rolls-Royce Merlin XX engines in an attempt to alleviate the demand on Bristol Hercules engines which were required for Short Stirling bombers, achieved a speed of 330 mph (531 km/h) and a range of 1 500 miles (2 414 km).

Notes on the finish
Beaufighter T3137 was supposed to have been finished in the standard scheme for overseas operations. In fact it wore a somewhat faded Temperate Sea scheme in which AM Sky Blue (which was even paler than AM Sky) was used instead of the prescribed AM Azure for the undersides. The demarcation line differed on the nacelles. The 789 Squadron code (W8) and the individual aircraft identification letter (R) were in Yellow, as were the spinners.

The Hellcats of 896 Squadron were finished in the Temperate Sea scheme, but had a washed-out appearance due to ultra-violet exposure. Because of this, the colours seemed to merge, while the Sky had faded to a dirty grey. Standard South East Asia Command roundels were worn, while the unit code (B7) and individual aircraft codes were painted in White.

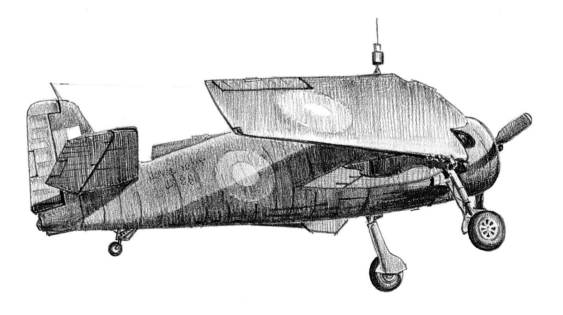

A Grumman Hellcat of 881 Squadron being hoisted aboard HMS Indefatigable *in Cape Town docks in 1946.*

A Bristol Beaufighter is flanked by Grumman Hellcats over Algoa Bay on a hot afternoon. The Port Elizabeth Airfield is situated to the left above the harbour and St Albans this side of the Lady's Slipper mountain above the nose of Hellcat B 7B.

Fairey Swordfish II

Fairey Swordfish Is and IIs were operated by 726 Squadron at Durban and 789 Squadron at Cape Town. One of these (HS256 of 726 Squadron) was transferred to Wingfield when the Durban unit disbanded. Purchased by a private company in 1947, it was stored in a hangar at Youngsfield in first class condition, displaying its original Fleet Air Arm colours, but in 1955 this valuable aircraft was accidentally destroyed by fire.

Notes on the finish
The Temperate Sea scheme was applied without shadow shading on the lower wings, while the AM Sky undersides (which showed very little discolouration) were separated from the upper surfaces by a wavy line which sloped down from the tailplane. (This was standard on the Swordfish.) B and C1 roundels and standard fin flashes painted in the correct, unfaded colours were worn. The serial number was stencilled in Black. The cockpit had Black instrument panels and all internal surfaces were standard AM Grey-green.

A Fairey Swordfish reflects the early morning sun over Algoa Bay.

Port Elizabeth Airfield

In April 1945 the Port Elizabeth Airfield was at the peak of its tremendous wartime expansion. Although the war in Europe had ended, operations against the Japanese were on the increase.

This panoramic portrayal of the airfield on Sunday, 22 April 1945 illustrates two North American Harvards from 11 Operational Training Unit (which was fully operational at the time) going round to land into a light north-west berg wind. On the ground are 21 Grumman F6F Hellcat FB IIs of 896 Squadron, Fleet Air Arm, which had just landed after a flight from Wingfield en route to Durban and the Pacific.

Apart from placing the airfield in its proper relationship to the city and bay, important developments of the airfield itself can also be seen. On the north boundary the original pre-war hangar and access road past Victoria Park are clearly visible, while on the south side (at the bottom of the painting) the red-roofed hangar originally used by 33 Flight is shown surrounded by the symmetrically arranged hangars of 42 Air School. About a year after the establishment of the Air School, 7 Air Depot was built on the north-east side of the field. A separate air base in its own right, known as Driftsands, it became the post-war Port Elizabeth Air Force Base. In 1951 the airfield was rebuilt with runways and became known as the Port Elizabeth Airport and later as H. F. Verwoerd Airport.

The Port Elizabeth Airfield, also often referred to as South End or Driftsands, was a typical military airfield with an approach from any direction. In addition it had the advantage of being near the city centre, harbour and residential areas. For a lad besotted by aircraft (as I was), the atmosphere and excitement of such an environment evoked a never-to-be-forgotten fascination. There were the smells, such as the resinous aroma of pines, the fragrance of dill crushed underfoot and that of freshly-cut grass mixed with burnt high-octane fuel and cellulose. After the brief showers of summer the smell of hundreds of doped fabric and timber airframes drying in the sun also pervaded the area.

The sounds, too, created a romantic setting. Apart from the aircraft, each with a dominant characteristic tonal variation to its engine noise, the sounds varied from the familiar shrieking of the 'kiewietjies' (crowned plovers) and loud playful duets of 'kok-o-viks' to the clattering of the narrow-guage locomotive and the echo of its shrill whistle through the pine and bluegum plantations along the track. On calm, crisp autumn and winter evenings, when the day's flying was done and the last strains of the parade's bugle band had died down, the airfield's heartbeat became audible, often in the form of the constant monotonous drone of an aircraft engine running on the test-bed at 7 AD, sometimes accompanied by the nearby call of nightjars.

An idea of the activity at the airfield can be gained by listing the aircraft on the base during this particular Sunday. The Harvards of 11 OTU are on the left of the small hangar along the north boundary, while to the right are the Hawker Hurricanes and the last Curtiss Kittyhawk of this unit's 'B' Squadron. Aircraft associated with 7 AD are (on the far right) five Lockheed PV-1 Venturas of 17 Squadron recently arrived from the Mediterranean Theatre, Fairey Battle TTs, Miles Masters, a de Havilland Dominie, Hurricanes and a polished-metal Kittyhawk. In the foreground are the aircraft of 42 AS: Avro Ansons, Airspeed Oxfords, Battles, B-34 and PV-1 Venturas, Harvards and grounded Northrop Nomads, Hawker Audaxes and Masters as well as various impressed light planes awaiting destruction. In front of the control tower are parked the Hellcats of 896 Squadron and a Bristol Beaufighter II of 789 Squadron, Fleet Air Arm.

Harvards Nos 7311 and 7153 are interesting examples from 11 OTU. Finished in polished natural metal, they had Yellow rectangles and Black serial numbers positioned further aft than the position adopted during the post-war years. No 7311 wore standard Yellow wing bands without the serial number, while No 7153 had overall Yellow outer wing panels which displayed the serial number very roughly applied with a spray-gun. Both aircraft had B and C1 roundels, with A-type roundels on their undersides.

Two North American Harvards banking over the Port Elizabeth Airfield in April 1945. The suburb of Walmer is on the left and South End, the city centre and Algoa Bay can be seen on the right.

Bristol Beaufighter II

A Bristol Beaufighter banks over the Algoa Bay shoreline with Cape Recife in the background.

At least two Bristol Beaufighter IIs were operated along the South African coast by 726 and 789 Fleet Requirement Units. One of these (T3137) led 896 Squadron's Grumman F6F Hellcats from Wingfield to Durban. The other (T3099, W9Q) also served with 789 FRU (it was recorded in an all-metal finish in mid-1945) and had unusual markings, with a Black code in place of the fuselage roundel and the 789 FRU crest on the fin. B roundels were retained on the wing upper surfaces and C roundels underneath, and there were matt Black anti-glare panels on the nacelles and nose.

Two mysterious Beaufighter IIs were seen at a distance in April and July 1945. One could have been T3099 in service with 726 FRU. It had the prescribed Azure undersides with Temperate Sea scheme top surfaces, and White spinners.

Another had an overall natural metal finish with camouflaged decking, and was also possibly T3099, this time with its camouflage partially removed after joining the complement of 789 FRU: at the time such unofficial decisions were often taken.

Grumman F6F Hellcat F II

The last Fleet Air Arm Grumman Hellcat squadron formed at Wingfield (881 Squadron, with Hellcat F IIs) was to have operated with the 12th Carrier Air Group in the British Pacific Fleet. Shortly before sailing for the East, however, Japan surrendered. The unit was therefore disbanded and the personnel returned home, leaving their aircraft behind.

In February 1946 HMS *Indefatigable* docked in Cape Town bound for Britain, and 30 Hellcats (with wings folded) were hoisted onto her flight deck after being towed from Wingfield. When *Indefatigable* sailed, the Supermarine Seafires of 24 Naval Fighter Wing were stowed below deck, and the Hellcats above, possibly for dumping at sea.

Notes on the finish
In June 1944 US Specification SR-2e prescribed that all carrier-based aircraft were to be finished in Glossy Sea Blue (FS 15042) overall. Most of the later deliveries of Hellcats wore this blue scheme, which was retained by the FAA. Hellcat JX981 of 881 Squadron wore South East Asia Command roundels, the matt Blue of which was one of the SAAF colours – a paler shade when contrasted with the Glossy Sea Blue.

An 881 Squadron Grumman Hellcat and a Fairey Barracuda from HMS Colossus over the Cape Peninsula. The warm summer atmosphere is typical of the Cape.

De Havilland 98 Mosquito XVI

With a thunderous roar from its Rolls-Royce Merlin engines, a de Havilland Mosquito sweeps over East London at rooftop level during a visit in 1945.

In November 1945 East Londoners were amazed to hear the thunderous roar of Rolls-Royce Merlin engines 'travelling up Oxford Street'. Those north of the central business district glimpsed a de Havilland Mosquito, in combat colours, bank to starboard and disappear in an easterly direction at rooftop level. A vision of the overall Blue finish, Red-on-White striped fin, flashing Yellow spinners and Black-and-White stripes stayed with the viewers as the engine note diminished into a distant droning rumble.

It was all merely a matter of the heart: Lieuts D. Hoskin and P. Stofberg of 60 Photographic Reconnaisance Squadron (SAAF), then based at Bloemspruit, had fiancées in East London, and had arranged for permission to fly to the coast as a 'test' after swinging the machines' compasses. Before the return flight to Bloemfontein, Lieut Hoskin promised his young lady (a tracer in the East London City Engineers' Department) that they would fly along Oxford Street at the same height as the City Hall clock!

The SAAF's association with the Mosquito goes back to 1943, when 60 Squadron, then equipped with Martin Baltimores, received their first two Mosquitoes. These were Mk II fighters which were modified, as an interim measure, for photo-reconnaisance duties 'in the field' at the instigation of Field Marshal Montgomery to assist in his North African campaign. By the time the Allies moved into Italy, the unit was equipped with Mosquito IXs designed specifically for photographic reconnaissance. In addition the unit had examples of the not-so-successfully pressurised Mosquito XVI, and these aircraft were used to carry out long-range strategic reconnaissance operations over South Germany and the Balkans.

One of many successful flights over the Ploesti oil fields was carried out by Lieut A. Miller, son of Maj Allister Miller, the founder of Union Airways. However, during 1944 he and his navigator failed to return from a mission, possibly becoming victims of a Messerschmitt Me 262 jet fighter. The opposition the unarmed aircraft encountered on these long-range missions could be pretty hair-raising, and can be typified by the flight of Capt 'Pi' Pienaar and Lieut Lockhart-Ross over South Germany in August 1944. During this flight they were surprised by a Messerschmitt Me 262 which made nine passes before breaking off the engagement when they reached cloud cover. The only evasive action Capt Pienaar could take during the struggle was to bank sharply to the right, and all the while they were regularly struck by cannon fire which demolished large sections of the port wing, tailplane and rudder. Still, they made it back to base – and how many aircraft of a similar size, but constructed of metal, could have taken such punishment?

R BELLIN © 87

One of those deadly 30-mm shells was capable of breaking a Spitfire's back.

For a time 60 Squadron was the only reconnaissance unit operating across the Alps, and it established an outstanding record for 'delivering the goods' in keeping with their motto 'We show the way'. With the cessation of hostilities the unit assisted the RAF in a survey of Italy and Greece, prior to returning to the Union with their aircraft (a gift from the British Government). Arriving at Zwartkop Air Base in August 1945, the aircraft, with their Photo Reconnaissance Unit Blue finishes and various trim colours, attracted a great deal of attention. Langebaanweg was intended to be the squadron's post-war base, but proved unsatisfactory because of the dampness and humidity at the coast, and so the squadron was transferred to Bloemspruit.

The Mosquito XVI was a beautifully clean aircraft, and the type represented the pinnacle in design and production of timber-built warplanes. By any standards it proved remarkably successful. Powered by two Rolls-Royce Merlin 72/73 or 76/77 engines of 1 680 or 1 710 hp (1 260 or 1 280 kW), it attained a maximum speed of 415 mph (668 km/h) at 28 000 ft (8 534 m). Except for the Messerschmitt Me 262, most aircraft had great difficulty in intercepting a Mosquito IX or XVI reconnaisance plane at high altitude.

Notes on the finish
The de Havilland Mosquitoes of 60 Squadron wore the standard RAF PRU Blue finish. By the time they flew down to the Union, this had become washed out on the upper surfaces, due to ultra-violet breakdown. Black and White fuselage 'invasion stripes' were worn by most aircraft, and a few had wing stripes as well. The spinners were Red or Yellow according to the flight to which the aircraft belonged. Mosquito RG129 was an impressive example with the Red-and-White diagonal fin and rudder stripes worn to avoid mistaking the Mosquito for a Messerschmitt Me 410. Some machines had no markings apart from the serial number and sometimes a code letter. The original RAF B-type roundels were changed to rough C-type roundels with Orange centres.

Vought F4U Corsair IV

HMS *Colossus* docked at Simon's Town in January 1946 after a spell in the Far East, and on board was the 14th Carrier Air Group, comprising 1846 Squadron (Vought Corsairs) and 827 Squadron (Fairey Barracudas). During the two-and-a-half month refit the Corsair IVs (FG-ID versions built by Goodyear), carried out exercises from their temporary base at Wingfield prior to their return to the United Kingdom.

Notes on the finish
The overall United States Glossy Sea Blue finish showed signs of wear, especially in the form of scratches on the wings. Insignia were the large South East Asia Command type with rectangles on both sides to match the US layout. The earlier system of codes had been replaced by a carrier identification letter (in this case D) on the fin, while an individual aircraft number was positioned ahead of the fuselage roundel. This method has remained in use with the Fleet Air Arm up to the present. Corsair No 117 (KD750) had a large reproduction of the fairy tale character 'Mother Goose' painted on the nose behind the cooling gills, which was rare for FAA aircraft.

Two Vought Corsairs fly over Cape Town in January 1946. The new form of carrier code and number can clearly be seen.

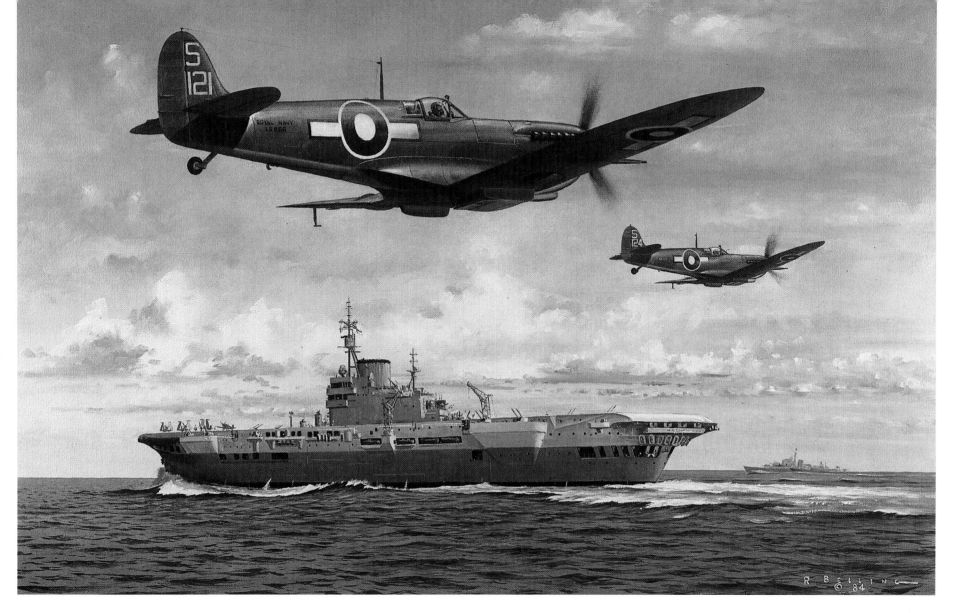

Supermarine Seafires over HMS Indefatigable, *steaming into Algoa Bay in February 1946.*

Supermarine Seafire III

On the morning of 18 February 1946 HMS *Indefatigable* unexpectedly arrived in Algoa Bay, signalling the port authorities that she would not dock, but intended carrying out flying exercises in the area during the day. Later 22 of her Supermarine Seafire IIIs took off to fly over the city, and the aircraft in their unfamiliar markings were an impressive sight, which was reinforced by the familiar drone of their Rolls-Royce Merlin engines.

They were from 887 and 894 Squadrons, comprising the 24th Naval Fighter Wing, and had been in the thick of combat at the end of World War II, a few months earlier.

On 15 August 1945, for example, aircraft from these squadrons were escorting Fairey Firefly Is and Grumman Avengers attacking a chemical factory on the shores of Odaki Bay near Tokyo. They intercepted Mitsubishi A6M 'Zeros' attempting to engage the Avengers,

and in the ensuing battle the Seafires shot down seven Japanese machines for the loss of one aircraft from 894 Squadron. When they returned to *Indefatigable*, the crews were informed that the war had ended a few minutes earlier. It was fitting that the navalized version of the Spitfire should have been victorious in what was possibly the last aerial combat of World War II.

Sadly though, back in Port Elizabeth the wing recorded their last casualty. As they were landing aboard the carrier off St Croix Island in Algoa Bay, Sub-Lieut Hatton's Seafire drifted to port, went over the side and sank, taking the pilot with it.

After calling at Cape Town, *Indefatigable*, now with the Grumman Hellcats of 881 Squadron on board, sailed to the United Kingdom, where 887 and 894 Squadrons were disbanded. The demise of these squadrons also meant the departure of the Seafire from the FAA. However, a twist of fate was to determine that the Seafire III's last combat was to be back in the Far East. In March 1946 refurbished FAA Seafire IIIs were delivered to the French Aéronavale as their first post-war fleet fighters. One squadron each of Seafires and Douglas Dauntlesses equipped the newly-acquired HMS *Colossus*, renamed *Arromanches*, which was stationed in French Indo-China. In 1948-1949 they operated against rebels from Saigon.

The Seafire III, fitted with a 1 470 hp (1 100 kW) Rolls-Royce Merlin engine, had a maximum speed of 352 mph (566 km/h), climbed to 20 000 ft (6 096 m) in 8,1 minutes and had a range of 465 miles (748 km). With folding wings, four-bladed airscrew and Aero-Vee filter, it resembled the Spitfire IX, but the asymetric radiator and oil cooler identified it as a navalized Spitfire V.

Notes on the finish

When HMS *Indefatigable* passed through the Suez Canal in November 1944 en route to the Pacific, her Seafires of 887 and 894 Squadrons were finished in the standard Temperate Sea scheme (although some were finished in the RAF fighter scheme) with B, C and C1 roundels and the squadron codes H5 and H6. By the time they went into action, the standard roundels were replaced by small South East Asia Command insignia. During 1945 large SEAC roundels with white surrounds and rectangles to coincide with United States aircraft were introduced. The codes were replaced by the ship's letter and aircraft number. The letter S was placed on the fin, but the large fuselage insignia left no space for the number, which was also painted on the fin, below the S. Seafire S124 was an interesting example, for when it was overhauled, the Dark Slate Grey was overpainted Extra Dark Sea Grey, while the serial number NN185 had mistakenly been replaced with a Yellow MM185, which was a Mosquito number.

Avro Lancaster I

On its return to the United Kingdom during April 1945, Lancaster PD328 'Aries' (see p 91) underwent a modification programme. In May it reappeared in a natural metal finish, and fairings to the nose and tail gave it the appearance of a Lancastrian. With a special long-range tank in the bomb bay and a new Lincoln-type undercarriage, 'Aries' undertook flights over the geographic and magnetic north poles as well as to Canada in June 1945. It also arrived at Cape Town on 17 January 1946 while on a long-range navigation flight, during which it had set a new record from the UK to Cape Town, which was one of 29 areas the aircraft visited.

Notes on the finish

After the camouflage was removed, the natural metal skinning of Lancaster PD328 was polished, which accentuated the somewhat rough rivet and frame lines. The name 'Aries' painted in Black on the nose was placed further forward than previously, and the C and C1 roundels with White rectangles were the same as when it flew to South Africa in 1945.

Avro Lancaster 'Aries' flying over heavy cloud near Cape Town in January 1946.

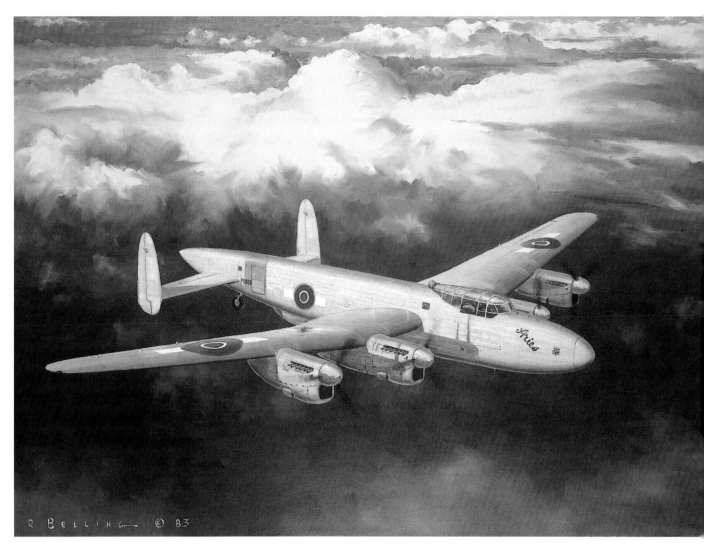

R BELLING © 83

Hawker Hurricane II

A post-war Hawker Hurricane flying against a cloudy, cold background.

When II Operational Training Unit disbanded after the war, a number of Hawker Hurricanes were overhauled, with the intention that they be used as interim fighters until the arrival of Supermarine Spitfire IXs. Five of these aircraft gave a memorable display over Pretoria and Johannesburg on 14 September 1946 to commemorate Battle of Britain Day.

During 1946 one of these (No 5336) called at Port Elizabeth. Another (No 5214) was for many years stored in the historical hangar at Central Flying School Dunnottar, together with the SAAF's Messerschmitt Me 262, Focke Wulf Fw 190 and Fieseler Fi 156 Storch. Although intended for the SAAF Museum, it was unfortunately accidently demolished.

Notes on the finish

These, the last Hurricanes to serve with the SAAF, were finished in what seems to have been a selected post-war scheme of BS Dark Earth upper surfaces and Sky undersides, with a large serial number applied in White aft of the fuselage roundel. C and CI roundels were worn, with fin flashes of non-standard proportions. The finish was generally of a high standard although, as was the case with Lockheed Venturas, the Sky was incongruous.

De Havilland 98 Mosquito XVI

Less than a year after their arrival in the Union, the historical combat colouring of 60 Squadron's Mosquitoes had been replaced by the more practical Silver finish which was intended to counter the damaging effect of the intense sun on timber-built aircraft. As was the case with Airspeed Oxfords and Miles Masters, however, the service life of the Mosquitoes was limited. After a fatal crash in June 1947, in fact, all SAAF Mosquitoes were grounded. Unfortunately the only remaining example of this remarkable aircraft in the Republic, a Mosquito PR IX of 60 Squadron housed in the South African National Museum of Military History, is poorly finished and requires a great deal of restoration before it can go on display as an authentic representative of this famous type. Imagine, though, a beautifully restored de Havilland 9 and a Mosquito side by side in authentic finishes.

Notes on the finish
Mosquito No 4802 was finished in Silver overall and had A-type roundels on the fuselage and upper wing surfaces and a Black serial number on the undersides. A space was left between the 8 and 0 of the number to accommodate long-range tanks. The 60 Squadron code (JS) and the aircraft letter (Q) were in Red. The aircraft had Black spinners, Dark Green anti-glare panels and a White sunshield on a section of the canopy, and looked considerably different from when it operated over Germany.

Shortly before being scrapped, a de Havilland Mosquito flies over Pretoria as the low early-evening sun touches the higher clouds.

Douglas C-47 Dakota

Carrying Field Marshal Bernard Montgomery as a distinguished passenger, this Douglas Dakota is about to touch down at the Port Elizabeth Airfield on 26 November 1947.

On 26 November 1947 the attractive musical reverberating rumble of Pratt & Whitney engines – reminiscent of the Consolidated Catalina – heralded the arrival of a Douglas C-47 Dakota, which gracefully came in to carry out a perfect landing at the Port Elizabeth Airfield. The beautifully polished natural metal finish betrayed the role of this aircraft (No 6852) as that of a VIP transport. On board was Field Marshal Bernard Montgomery, who was touring various South African cities and military bases to meet many of the men who had served under him during the Desert Campaign. Later named 'Fleur', this aircraft

served for many years as a transport for Chiefs of Staff. Currently camouflaged, it is still operated by the SAAF more than forty years later.

The Dakota story began in 1935 when American Airlines' president C. R. Smith requested that Douglas redesign the DC-2 then in airline service with a wide body and longer range to replace the airline's Condor 'Sleeper' biplanes, the only aircraft then suited to fly the long routes across the United States from coast to coast. In the process the legendary Douglas Commercial Three was born.

By the time World War II broke out, the successful DC-3 airliner was adopted by the

US as their standard military transport, and ultimately it was built in greater numbers than any other trooper. It was employed in every combat area of World War II, and enjoyed an operational life that continues to this day, especially in the Republic.

The SAAF received their first Dakotas in 1943, and they operated with 28 and 44 Squadrons in the Mediterranean Theatre. With the cessation of hostilities they flew a shuttle service, ferrying troops back to the Union. During 1948-1949 28 Squadron took part in the Berlin Airlift for more than six months, using RAF machines.

Nicknamed 'Gooney Bird', this remarkable aircraft still serves the SAAF who, with their usual care, seem to get more out of their aircraft than most Air Forces. When 35 Squadron retired their Avro Shackletons,

Dakotas were modified to carry out limited maritime patrols, earning themselves the new nickname 'Dackleton'.

Designated C-47 Skytrain by the US Air Force and Dakota by the RAF, there were numerous other main-run designations, such as C-48 through C-53 (Skytrooper), as well as C-68, C-84 and C-117. Powered by twin 1 200 hp Pratt & Whitney R-1830 engines, the C-47 had a maximum speed of 230 mph (370 km/h), climbed at 1 000 ft/min to a ceiling of 24 000 ft (7 315 m) and had a range of 1 600 miles (2 575 km).

Notes on the finish
All Allied Dakotas originally flew in the standard United States scheme of Olive Drab (FS 34087 – both versions) upper surfaces and Neutral Gray (FS 36118 Sea Gray) undersides. The top surface colour varied a great deal due to fading and wear and also because there were two versions of the Olive Drab. Although both are referred to as FS 34087, the most common is very much like BS Dark Green, whereas the other tended to be like Dark Earth, but not quite as brown.

When SAAF Dakotas were repainted, the Dark Green, Dark Earth and Azure scheme was used, although a number of machines had Dark Green overall upper surfaces. In 1946 one of the first Dakotas to visit the Port Elizabeth Airfield wore a Dark Green and Azure finish with a wavy separation line. The clean, newly-applied finish contrasted with the old B and C1 roundels, which were faded, although the underside serial number and A-type roundels were freshly painted.

Shortly after the war the camouflage was removed from SAAF transport aircraft. One of these (No 6852) wore its serial number far aft, directly above the tailwheel. It had A-type roundels and standard fin flashes, as well as matt Ultramarine anti-glare panels. In 1947, when the RAF adopted the D-type roundel, the SAAF followed suit, and also followed the RAF style and sizes in regard to serial numbers. When the Springbok insignia were introduced during the 1950s, the fuselage decking of Dakota No 6852, now named 'Fleur', was painted white and separated from the polished skinning by an Insignia Blue stripe.

A Lockheed B-34 Ventura flies low over South End after taking off from the Port Elizabeth Airfield on a wintry morning.

Lockheed B-34 Ventura

As part of its post-war re-organisation, the SAAF adopted the Lockheed Ventura as a medium bomber (B-34) and inshore maritime patrol aircraft (PV-1) to support the Short Sunderlands of 35 Squadron. These colourful machines, with the characteristic deep rumble from their powerful engines, played an important role in South African aviation for more than 17 years. When they were finally retired in December 1959, they had seen longer service in the SAAF than in any other country's air force.

Notes on the finish
During 1947 a B-34 Ventura (No 6019) occasionally seen at the Port Elizabeth Airfield was finished with Dark Sea Grey upper surfaces and Black undersides. The C and C1 roundels and large White fuselage serial number were the same as seen on the post-war Hurricanes. Generally this scheme conformed to the night coastal reconnaisance finish adopted by the RAF in 1944.

Silhouetted against the morning sunlight, Field Marshal Jan Smuts' personal Avro York banks over Port Elizabeth with the harbour visible.

Avro York

In 1947 Field Marshal Jan Smuts' Avro York (No 4999 – 'Oubaas') arrived at St Albans, the large fuselage clearly distinguishing the type from the slim Lancaster. Most early production examples of this aircraft became VIP transports: Winston Churchill used the third production aircraft, while MW107 became Field Marshal Smuts' personal transport. When the war ended, it was transferred to the SAAF as No 4999.

Determined to exploit the Lancaster's long range and load capacity, Avro retained the bomber's wings, tail unit, engines and undercarriage, but designed a new large square-sectioned fuselage for maximum capacity. The prototype flew in the remarkably short time of five months after the drawings were issued to the experimental shop. Because the type had no heating or extensive insulation, passengers were issued with blankets. The

effects of the four 1 620 hp (1 210 kW) Rolls-Royce Merlin T24 engines on the passengers' eardrums, however, took some time to wear off after long flights. The York C I had a maximum speed of 298 mph (480 km/h), a ceiling of 26 000 ft (7 925 m) and a range of 2 700 miles (4 345 km). York No 4999 was sold to Tropic Airways in 1952.

Notes on the finish
When originally built, York MW107 should have conformed to the standard RAF communications finish of Temperate Land scheme top surfaces and Yellow undersides. Because SAAF transports had Sky undersides, the Yellow would have been changed. The camouflage of No 4999 was removed after the war. With a polished metal finish, it wore A-type roundels on all surfaces and standard fin flashes on the outer surfaces. The serial number on the undersides and rear fuselage were in Black. The Prime Minister's pennant was painted below the cockpit.

Short Sunderland V

When Short Sunderlands flew patrols along the coast to the accompaniment of the rumble of their four Pratt & Whitney Twin Wasp engines, their large white ship-like forms seemed to sail past rather than fly.

In April 1945 35 Squadron replaced their Consolidated Catalinas with sixteen Sunderland GR Vs intended for service in the Far East. Based at Congella, Durban, and flying from St Lucia and Langebaan as well, they established a high standard of operations. On 16 February 1947 a special flight was undertaken to make contact with the battleship HMS *Vanguard*, with the Royal Family on board, at the start of their tour of South Africa. During August 1957 the SAAF's Sunderlands ceased flying and Congella was closed as a flying boat base when the unit moved to new accommodation at Ysterplaat, operating new Avro Shackletons.

Built as a military development of the successful 'C' Class Empire Flying Boat, the Sunderland was a remarkably sound design which proved to be one of the best flying boats of World War II, with a very good anti-U-boat record. The Sunderland I and III had Bristol Pegasus engines. The Sunderland IV, with Bristol Hercules engines, did not go into production, but was the most attractive version, with beautifully cowled engines, spinners and a shapely dorsal fin. A civil version, the Solent, became a popular post-war flying boat and continued the pre-war 'C' class service (see p 55). The design had come full circle. Initially an interim model, the Mk V, powered by 1 200 hp (900 kW) Pratt & Whitney Twin Wasp engines, became the final version, serving with a number of air arms during the post-war years. Fitted with air-to-surface vessel radar radomes under the wings it achieved a maximum speed of 213 mph (343 km/h), a range of 2 980 miles (4 795 km) and an endurance of 13½ hours.

Notes on the finish
On delivery 35 Squadron's Sunderlands were finished according to the British AM instruc-

tion of October 1944 for aircraft on coastal duties, with upper surfaces finished in Extra Dark Sea Grey, undersides in gloss White and sides (including nacelles) in matt White. In the early 1950s the RAF standardised the top surface finish to Medium Sea Grey, but the SAAF retained their original colours. The hull undersides were natural metal with a protective coating, but this became very stained as it collected oil and other dirt from the waters of Durban harbour. C and C1 roundels and 36 x 24 in (915 x 610 mm) fin flashes were worn, but there were no roundels on the undersides. The squadron code (RB) was worn with original RAF serial numbers until the SAAF numbers were applied. In the early 1950s Springbok roundels were introduced on all surfaces and the SAAF serial number was painted on the undersides.

Left above: *A Short Sunderland throws up spray as it 'digs in' after its landing run in Durban Bay.*

Left: *A Sunderland circles* HMS Vanguard *and the cruiser* HMS Nigeria − *flagship of the South Atlantic Station − in February 1947.*

Supermarine Spitfire IX

During April 1947 the first batch of 136 Supermarine Spitfire IXs for the SAAF was delivered from the United Kingdom. The aircraft were flown to Cairo by RAF crews, from where the SAAF flew them to Pretoria. Although referred to as HF IXe's, there were variations depending on the date of production. Some early models (originally Mk Vs returned to Castle Bromwich and rebuilt as Mk IXs) betrayed their vintage by their round-headed rear fuselage rivetting. Although most were fitted with the later pointed rudder, a few retained the rounded design. The standard bubble canopy was fitted to many, but late models had the cut-down rear fuselage with teardrop transparency. While in SAAF service

they underwent a number of further minor modifications. As the standard front-line fighter, Spitfires equipped 1 and 2 Squadrons, as well as 60 Squadron after modifications for photographic operations. Many were based at Langebaanweg where, in addition to general operational training, aircrews preparing to go to Korea received combat training.

By 1954 these beautiful machines were grounded to make way for the de Havilland Vampire. Sadly the restoration of the unique SAAF examples is marked by a series of lost opportunities and cases of individual selfishness which has left only one machine in the care of the SAAF Museum.

Fitted with the Rolls-Royce Merlin 63, 66

Above: *A post-war Supermarine Spitfire in an early camouflage scheme. Note the Dark Green patch on the nose.*

Right: *A 60 Squadron Spitfire against the background of a threatening thunderhead. Note the small D-type roundels.*

or 70 engine of 1 700 hp (1 270 kW), the Spitfire IX had a maximum speed of 408-416 mph (657-669 km/h), climbed to 20 000 ft (6 096 m) in 6,4 mins, and had a ceiling of 43 000 ft (13 106 m) and a range of 434 miles (698 km) or 980 (1 577 km) with a long-range tank. Apart from their two 20-mm cannon and two .5 inch machine guns, most of the operational aircraft were fitted with bomb racks and four zero-length rocket rails for a ground attack role. With a large Gyro gunsight, large throttle control lever and cluttered control column with firing buttons for the various armaments, the cluttered cockpit looked more like that of a Spitfire XXII or Seafire 47 than that of a Spitfire IX.

Notes on the finish
When delivered, the Spitfires were finished in the RAF scheme of Dark Green, Ocean Grey and Medium Sea Grey with a Sky spinner and rear fuselage band. The first aircraft to equip 1 Squadron were overhauled and repainted in the same scheme as the Hurricanes – Dark Earth overall with Sky undersides. Spitfire AX-A (No 5502) wore its code letters in Yellow and had C and C1 roundels and 24 x 24 in (610 x 610 mm) fin flashes.

Soon afterwards, however, the SAAF adopted the RAF scheme, but without the Sky trim. With their Dark Green, Ocean Grey and Medium Sea Grey finish 1 Squadron aircraft retained their Yellow code letters, spinners and wing leading edge. The C roundels gave way to the 36 in (915 mm) D-type in six positions, together with 24 x 24 in (610 x 610 mm) fin flashes with BS Aircraft Blue. Serial numbers were repeated on the undersides in accordance with British dimensions. Spitfire AX-M (No 5516) with a teardrop canopy was a good example (p 109).

Above: *A Spitfire performing a loop at high altitude. Note the revised roundels and the incorrectly applied fin flash colours.*

Left: *The beautiful lines and impression of speed created by this Spitfire complement the formation of a swept thunderhead.*

Wearing the final version of its camouflage scheme, a Spitfire fires a salvo of 60-lb rockets as the pilot trains for action in the Korean conflict.

Two of 1 Squadron's machines were interesting. Spitfires AX-Y and AX-N (with the standard finish) had small 18 in (457 mm) C1-type roundels in the six positions, although they were positioned far inboard on the wings. The Blue of the 18 x 12 in (457 x 305 mm) fin flashes on AX-Y was mistakenly painted on the forward side (see p 109).

During 1950 a revised camouflage was introduced. Top surfaces were painted in semi-gloss Extra Dark Sea Grey and the undersides in Medium Sea Grey, which was more in keeping with present colours. Squadron codes were eliminated and 24 in (610 mm) D-type roundels were worn in the six positions, but moved near to the wingtips to allow

for the positioning of a smaller underwing serial number. The fin flashes were reduced to 21 x 24 in (533 x 610 mm). Shortly afterwards the Springbok motif was introduced, but the roundels remained the same excepting that an Orange stencilled Springbok was added in place of the inner circle.

R BELLING © 85

Hawker Sea Fury

On 18 November 1948 an aircraft with pale undersides and grey decking arrived over Port Elizabeth, a smooth whistling purr emanating from its engine, and performed an impressive high speed roll. As it circled the Port Elizabeth Airfield to land, it was joined by seven others.

While the eight Hawker Sea Fury FB IIs from 802 Squadron came round in line astern to land, eight more machines arrived over the field. This time the accompanying sound was the droning crackle of Rolls-Royce Griffon engines as the Fairey Firefly FR IVs of 814 Squadron broke formation to join in the circuit. The 15th Carrier Air Group, based on HMS *Vengeance*, had arrived at Port Elizabeth to refuel. Together with 17 CAG aboard HMS *Theseus*, they called at South African ports while on a South Atlantic cruise.

In 1948 the Sea Fury and its United States counterpart the Grumman Bearcat represented the forefront of service naval fighter design. Both had powerful radial engines with installations reminiscent of the BMW layout in the Focke Wulf Fw 190. These popular aircraft served from 1947 to 1954, when some were relegated to Royal Navy Volunteer Reserve units until finally retired in 1957. On 9 August 1952, while operating from HMS *Ocean* during the Korean War, an 802 Squadron Sea Fury, flown by Lieut Carmichael, was credited with the destruction of a MiG-15 jet fighter.

Developed from the Hawker Typhoon via the Tempest, which it closely resembled, the Fury did not enter RAF service. The navalized version, however, became the Sea Fury. Although its predecessors to some extent maintained the original welded steel tubular frame of the biplane Hawker Fury and Hurricane, the Sea Fury had a semi-monocoque fuselage fitted with shapely reduced-span Tempest wings. Fitted with the 2 470 hp (1 850 kW) Bristol Centaurus engine, it had a speed of 460 mph (740 km/h), a climb rate of 4 320 ft/min (1 317 m/min) and a range of 700 miles (1 127 km). With this performance the Sea Fury could claim to be one of the few aircraft

to represent the peak of piston-engined operational fighters.

Notes on the finish
The standard finish for fleet fighters was Extra Dark Sea Grey top surfaces and Sky undersides and spinner. C and CI roundels and standard fin flashes in wartime Blue and Red were worn. The carrier code (a White letter Q) was painted on the fin, and the aircraft number (also in White) behind the fuselage roundel. Serial numbers were displayed under the wings.

One of the Sea Furies (No 109) was finished in the new naval aircraft scheme and made an interesting comparison with the others (see p 112). The undersides, fuselage flanks and vertical tail surfaces were Sky, and the upper surfaces, spinner and fuselage decking Extra Dark Sea Grey. D-type roundels in BS Aircraft Blue and BS Post Office Red were worn, but no fin flashes. The carrier code letter and aircraft serial numbers were in Black. All aircraft were finished with gloss paintwork, and were very well maintained, which left the colours sharp and clear.

A Hawker Sea Fury sweeps low over the Cape Recife lighthouse in November 1948.

A Fairey Firefly is kept company by two Hawker Sea Furies while flying from Durban to Port Elizabeth. Note the newly-introduced scheme on the top aircraft as compared with the earlier fighter and strike aircraft schemes on the others.

R BELLING © 86

Fairey Firefly FR IV

The Fairey Firefly FR IVs of 814 Squadron aboard HMS *Vengeance* were the anti-submarine strike and reconnaisance version of the Firefly I fleet fighter which saw considerable action in the Far East during the closing months of World War II. On the Mk IV the chin radiator of the Mk I made way for a chin like that of the North American P-51 Mustang, and in addition the Mk I's elliptical wings were cut square. Like the Sea Fury, they were among the most advanced aircraft of their type in 1948. Flying in the close support role from light fleet carriers during the

Korean conflict, Firefly IVs and Vs gave a good account of themselves on operations which included minelaying and shipping strikes. With good handling qualities, sound performance, versatility and exceptional reliability the Firefly was a popular Fleet Air Arm aircraft.

Powered by a 2 250 hp (1 680 kW) Rolls-Royce Griffon 74 engine, the Firefly IV had a maximum speed of 386 mph (621 km/h) and a range of 660 or 1 300 miles (1 062 or 2 092 km) depending on tankage. Apart from four 20-mm cannon, sixteen 60-lb (27 kg) rockets or two 1 000-lb (454 kg) bombs could be carried. Air-to-surface homing radar was housed in the starboard underwing radome fairing, and an auxiliary fuel tank occupied the port position.

Notes on the finish
Although finished in the wartime Temperate Sea scheme introduced in October 1944, which included C and C1 roundels, the high gloss finish, which was immaculately maintained, imbued the colours with a distinct sharpness as compared to the matt washed-out wartime finish. This variation is graphically illustrated by comparing the Bristol Beaufighter (see p 93) and Supermarine Seafire IIIs (p 100) with Firefly No 218 (Q, TW724). One machine (No 112) was partially painted in the new Extra Dark Sea Grey upper surface finish. D roundels were applied. All aircraft had the then fashionable large serial numbers on the undersides.

Lockheed PV-1 Ventura (VIP and TT)

Shortly after World War II a few Lockheed Venturas were modified as VIP transports to operate with 28 Squadron, reducing the flying time from Pretoria to Cape Town to just over three hours. After its conversion No 6487 (29 Squadron) was transferred to 28 Squadron in mid-1946. It had a polished natural metal finish, matt Ultramarine anti-glare nose and nacelle panels and (initially) A-type roundels.

During the early 1950s the Springbok roundel was introduced, and VIP aircraft were finished with White fuselage decking with Ultramarine separating stripes. Castle insignia were introduced prior to their retirement.

Another comparatively rare Ventura type were the post-war target tugs. The smooth fuselage topline was broken by the bulky winch and supporting structure. The aircraft were finished in the standard RAF overall Yellow with 36 in (915 mm) Black diagonal bands at an angle of 60° and 72 in (1 829 mm) wide on all surfaces. The stabilizer was Black and the elevators Yellow.

Ventura No 6481 was based at the Port Elizabeth Air Base for a short period during 1954 to undertake drogue-towing flights for maritime exercises off the coast. In 1960, when the Ventura disappeared from the scene, a Dakota was modified to continue the target tug duties. Apart from white decking, the same scheme was retained.

Above: *A Lockheed Ventura target tug off the Eastern Cape coast during 1954.*

Left: *Flying low over the Roman Rock bell bouy, a VIP Ventura faces a low westerly sun as it comes in over Algoa Bay.*

North American Harvard II

When 42 Air School, 11 Operational Training Unit and 7 Air Depot closed down at the end of World War II, the RAF flying school hangars became the property of the Port Elizabeth Municipality, which leased them to various civil organizations. A few survive to this day. They are rusting and overgrown by blue-gums, but are still in use as boat-building shops. Former 7 AD hangars became the post-war SAAF component of Eastern Province Command. In 1950-1951 the airfield was closed while two runways and new airport facilities were constructed, and St Albans had to be recommissioned to serve the city.

Shortly after Port Elizabeth Airport re-opened, the SADF initiated a Citizen Force pupil pilot training scheme. The local Flying Club maintained de Havilland Tiger Moths for primary training, and Capts Nick Carter and Phil Smulian, both former 42 AS pilots, were commissioned as instructors.

In July 1956 6 'City of Port Elizabeth' CF Squadron came into being, flying North American Harvard IIs. Apart from a break of two years, these aircraft played an important role in the city's aviation activities for 23 years and their familiar rasping whine could be heard almost every day.

Above: *The hangars of 42 Air School in 1988.*

Right: *A North American Harvard in the attractive finish introduced during the 1950s, shown against the backdrop of a watery winter sun.*

Opposite: *The last Harvard to serve with 6 Squadron flies over the Swartkops River in 1975.*

R BELLING © 86

In 1959 6 Squadron was disbanded due to economic measures, but reformed again in 1961, operating the Harvard II, III and T-6G. During the morning of 22 March 1975 6 Squadron's Harvards left Port Elizabeth for Central Flying School Dunnottar, as they were to be replaced by Impala Is. Harvard No 7621 remained at the Port Elizabeth Air Base, however, to undergo an overhaul. On 6 November 1975 Harvard No 7711 arrived with a second pilot on board, and at 14h30 Nos 7711 and 7621 flew low over the city to end the Harvard's direct association with Port Elizabeth after 32 years.

Notes on the finish

Although no post-war SAAF units were permanently based at Port Elizabeth before 1956, Lockheed Venturas, Douglas Dakotas and Harvards regularly visited there. The latter wore D-type roundels.

The first Harvards attached to 6 Squadron were finished in the standard post-war scheme of polished natural metal overall with Extra Dark Sea Grey applied to the wing upper surfaces and anti-glare panel. A Yellow rectangle with a Black border was positioned below the cockpit as background to the Black serial number – further forward than those on wartime machines. There were Yellow bands on the wings, fuselage and wingtips.

Springbok roundels replaced the earlier D-type originally worn with this scheme. One machine (No 7155) retained the wartime large Black serial number outlined with Yellow instead of placed on a Yellow rectangle. In 1957 Castle insignia replaced the Springbok insignia, and Glossy (Satin) Silver was adopted instead of natural metal.

In keeping with overseas trends, a revised scheme using Day-Glo was adopted for Harvards in 1960. The colour Fire Orange (SABS A46 or FS 28914) was chosen when Blaze Orange, which was the initial choice, proved, after tests, to be too difficult to maintain. The wing upper surfaces were finished in Extra Dark Sea Grey and there was a Yellow fuselage rectangle. The engine cowling, wing bands, top leading edge, stabiliser, fin and rear fuselage were finished in Day-Glo. The Castle insignia remained as before.

Flying through an early-morning haze, three Dassault Flamants are accompanied by a Junkers Ju 52/3m shortly after leaving Durban for Port Elizabeth.

Dassault MD.315 Flamant

During the early 1950s French aircraft regularly used facilities at the Port Elizabeth Air Base. During one such an occasion what at first looked like three Lockheed Venturas came in over the sea – but on closer inspection they turned out to be Dassault Flamants. As they circled, their long wings and the smooth crackle from their in-line engines distinguished them from the Ventura. Serving with the Armée de l'Air and based at Tananarive, Madagascar, they were on their way to Cape Town. While being refuelled, they were joined by a Junkers Ju 52/3m, the personal transport of the Commander-in-Chief, Indian Ocean Strategic Zone, who had also arrived at the base.

Designed as a light general-purpose transport for service mainly in French colonial territories, the Flamant was powered by two 600 hp (450 kW) Renault 12S engines (originally the German Argus As 411), and was the first post-war product produced by Marcel Dassault (formerly Bloch). Of conventional all-metal construction, the Flamant could carry 10 passengers at a maximum speed of 236 mph (380 km/h), and had a climb rate of near-

ly 1 000 ft/min (305 m/min) to a ceiling of 26 240 ft (7 998 m). It had a range of 755 miles (1 215 km).

Notes on the finish
In an overall natural polished metal finish, one of the aircraft (No 95) wore the code letter R on its outer fins, as well as standard French roundels of Cerulean Blue, White and Red with a thin Yellow outer ring, and full rudder flashes on all surfaces. The spinners were Red and the Escadrille 50 insignia (a charging bull on a red diamond) was painted on the nose. The Junkers Ju 52/3m was finished in Silver overall, wore the fin code letter F and displayed the usual insignia.

Avro Lancaster MR (Aéronavale)

Early in 1954 a familiar drone was heard as an attractive all-blue Avro Lancaster flew westwards over Port Elizabeth, followed shortly after by a second aircraft. They were French Aéronavale machines based in French African colonies, in this case Madagascar. Under the 1948 Western Union Agreement, the predecessor of the North Atlantic Treaty Organization, ex-RAF Lancasters were ordered to equip the Aéronavale, for which purpose 54 Lancaster Is and VIIs were virtually rebuilt. With their mid-upper turrets removed, additional fuel tanks fitted in the bomb bays, provision made for the installation of air-to-surface vessel radar equipment and the capability of carrying air/sea rescue life boats (of which six were supplied to the Aéronavale by Avro), they became effective maritime reconnaissance Lancasters. Delivered in 1952, they operated efficiently until replaced in 1964.

Notes on the finish
It was the intention of the French Navy to adopt the US Navy Sea Blue finish, but this was changed to a lighter shade (between FS 15080 and FS 15090), which gave the aircraft an attractive tropical appearance.

In line astern, two Avro Lancasters of the French Aéronavale fly over the Eastern Cape coast in 1954.

R BELLING © 83

Supermarine Spitfire IX

During November 1953 a lone Spitfire circled South End and came in to make its last landing, accompanied by the then rare sound of its Rolls-Royce Merlin engine. Soon afterwards it was wheeled into 6 Squadron's hangar and its flying days were over. The only Spitfire based at Port Elizabeth Air Base, it was used for ground instruction.

This last Spitfire to fly out of Ysterplaat (No 5593) was fitted with a long-range slipper tank, which gave it sufficient range for the pilot to make the most of his last flight in the type. It was flown by Cmdt 'Porky' Rich, who later became Officer Commanding Port Elizabeth Airbase. One of the last production Spitfire IXs with clipped wings, cut-down rear fuselage and teardrop canopy, it was equipped for ground attack with four zero-length rocket rails and bomb racks. In 1955, after the gunsight and armaments were removed, this beautiful aircraft was stripped and railed to Pretoria for scrapping.

Notes on the finish
Spitfire No 5593 was finished in the final scheme for SAAF Spitfires, with Extra Dark Sea Grey upper surfaces and Medium Sea Grey undersides, with 24 in (610 mm) Springbok roundels in six positions and 18 x 24 in (457 x 610 mm) fin flashes and an 8 in (203 mm) serial number. The spinner appeared to be Black, but in fact had a Dark Blue hue, and the sliding canopy frame was painted in zinc chromate. The finish was semi-gloss. The SAAF Museum are presently rebuilding the only remaining SAAF Spitfire, which should ultimately resemble No 5593.

Silhouetted against sunlight and clouds, a Supermarine Spitfire IX cruises over the Langebaan lagoon.

De Havilland 100 Vampire FB 9 and T 11

With a shriek from their de Havilland Goblin gas turbine engines, five de Havilland Vampire FB 9s flew over Port Elizabeth on 16 July 1954. The leader was No 237, flown by Capt 'Pikkie' Rautenbach, who landed at the Port Elizabeth Airport after a very low-level beat-up of the main runway. This was the first jet-powered aircraft to land at Port Elizabeth.

Ten Vampire FB 5s were initially delivered in 1950 to replace the Spitfire IXs of 1 Squadron. Chosen by the SAAF for its simplicity and ease of maintenance, the Vampire was constructed very much like its stablemate, the DH 103 Hornet. Although the wings, tail and booms were built of metal, the fuselage was built of timber, using the same method of construction as that of the DH Mosquito.

Subsequently another 40 machines, mostly FB 9s, were ordered to replace the remaining Spitfires. These reliable aircraft continued the tradition between the SAAF and de Havillands and served the SAAF well until they were replaced by Canadair Sabres in first-line units from 1956 onwards. They also operated with the Operational Air Schools at Langebaanweg and Pietersburg, until replaced by Impala 1s. Between 1952 and 1954 about 30 Vampire T 11s and T 55s were delivered as the standard multi-purpose advanced trainer for Vampire and later Sabre aircrews. Unlike the single-seaters, these marks were fitted with ejection seats.

Powered by a 3 100-lb thrust DH Goblin 2 engine, a maximum speed of 535 mph (861 km/h), a rate of climb of 4 000 ft/min (1 219 m/min), a combat ceiling of 40 000 ft (12 192 m) and a range of 1 170 miles (1 883 km) with long-range tanks was achieved. With four 20-mm cannon, four zero-length rocket rails and bombs in place of long-range tanks, the Vampire was an effective fighter-bomber replacement for the Spitfires.

Notes on the finish

Throughout their service with the SAAF all Vampires wore an overall finish of High Speed (Satin) Silver, which was very smooth, achieved with numerous protective coats of clear lacquer. In spite of the glossy finish, the general appearance was that of a grey. The Vampire 5s initially had D-type roundels, which were soon replaced by Springbok roundels. 1 Squadron machines wore the code letters AX on the nose in Black, while those of 2 Squadron had Red trim. Vampire No 237 from 2 Squadron had a Red nose, underwing tank trim, fin bullets and wing tips. No 228 had no trim, and No 235 only a Red nose. Shortly after the introduction of Castle insignia, Day-Glo wing and boom bands and nose panels were standardised. Until the use of Day-Glo, the two-seaters had Yellow RAF-type wing and boom bands.

Above left: A de Havilland Vampire FB 9 performs a low-level beat-up of the Port Elizabeth Airport on 16 July 1954 before becoming the first jet to land there.

Above: Vampire T 55s during exercises at altitude in 1955.

Westland HR 1 Dragonfly and Fairey Firefly AS 5

When the light fleet carrier HMS *Warrior* docked in Port Elizabeth in November 1954 on a goodwill visit, she had aboard 811 Squadron's Hawker Sea Fury FB 2s, 825 Squadron's Fairey Firefly AS 5s, and two Westland Dragonfly helicopters.

Unlike the same types aboard HMS *Vengeance* six years earlier, the aircraft were now obsolete, but they were in remarkably good condition, even though they had been in action against Malayan terrorists. Although the SAAF had operated three US-built Sikorsky

S-51s since 1948, the Dragonflies were the first fleet helicopters over the Eastern Cape.

Built by Westland, the Dragonfly (a British version of the Sikorsky S-51) was powered by a 550 hp (410 kW) Alvis Leonides 50 engine, and had a maximum speed of 103 mph (166 km/h) and was able to climb at nearly 1 000 ft/min (305 m/min). Serving as 'plane guard' during flying operations in place of the ageing Supermarine Walrus and Sea Otter seaplanes and destroyer 'guards', on that particular cruise they had up to that point rescued seven aircrew under operational conditions.

An airman being lifted from the sea by a Dragonfly 'plane guard'.

Notes on the finish

The Dragonflies were Silver overall with D-type roundels. The carrier code letter and serial numbers were Black.

The Sea Furies were finished in spotless high-gloss Extra Dark Sea Grey and Sky and wore Blue spinners and the carrier code letter J in Black on the fin. All aircraft were fitted with long-range tanks and bomb racks. Examples were Nos 112 (WF592), 113 (WF544) and 102 (WE725).

The Firefly 5s of 825 Squadron wore the same finish, but had Red spinners. Four machines showed a non-standard variation: their fins and rudders were Extra Dark Sea Grey instead of Sky, and the carrier code letter J on the fin was in White. One such example was the illustrated aircraft, No 290 (WB409).

R BELLING © 87

De Havilland 104 Devon

De Havilland's first post-war civil aircraft was the Dove (built to replace the Dragon Rapide), and the DH Devon C 1 was the military communications version of this aircraft. It was a beautifully-proportioned machine with a fin and rudder shape reminiscent of the Mosquito, a nose like that of the Vampire and an undercarriage that was virtually the same as that of this fighter. Nine Devons (Nos 101-109) were ordered by the SAAF in late 1949 and served with 28 Squadron's VIP flight until the mid-1960s.

Powered by two 340 hp (255 kW) DH Gipsy Queen engines in beautiful cowlings that also accommodated the undercarriage, the type had a maximum speed of 210 mph (338 km/h), a ceiling of 20 000 ft (6 096 m) and a range of 1 000 miles (1 609 km).

Notes on the finish
The overall finish was Satin Silver, and Springbok roundels were worn on all surfaces. The serial numbers (including those on the undersides) were in Black. With the introduction of Castle insignia, the older roundels were oversprayed with Silver which never matched the original paintwork.

The early-morning sun accentuates the graceful lines of a de Havilland Devon as it climbs away from Port Elizabeth.

Messerschmitt Me 262 B-1A/U1

Although an aircraft with no direct links to the SAAF, the Messerschmitt Me 262 sent to the Union in 1947 together with two other captured Luftwaffe machines as a gift from the British Government is arguably the Republic's most valuable aviation relic.

The South African example (Red 8, No 170-305) is unique in that it is the only remaining Me 262 nightfighter in the world. Operated by 10 Staffel of Nachtjagdgeschwader 11 – the world's first jet nightfighter unit, under command of Oberleutnant Kurt Welter – it took part in the night defence of Berlin at the end of World War II. Welter became the top-scoring jet ace of the war, with 28 victories – many of them intruder de Havilland Mosquitoes. The Messerschmitt Me 262 Schwalbe (Swallow), conceptually the most advanced aircraft to be put into service by any of the combatants during World War II, has a place in aviation history which allows one to trace an analogy between music and machine. What Beethoven's Eroica Symphony was to music, the Me 262 was to aviation – a powerful new statement on the order of the future. The Me 262 was tangible evidence that Germany was the first country to lay the groundwork for high-speed aeronautics.

As early as the late 1920s German scientists and engineers were evaluating streamlined shapes at very high speeds. In 1933 Adolph Busemann achieved velocities of 1,5 times the speed of sound using special equipment at Göttingen, and during a conference in Rome in 1935 he drew attention to the advantages of thin wing profiles and swept surfaces to postpone drag rise. It seems that he was not taken seriously, for only in 1945, when Germany was overrun, did the Allies rediscover the value of the remarkable research programmes and related projects. The Me 262 was an interim adaption of what was intended to follow – as a matter of fact the official manual for this advanced machine referred to it as conceived for easy production by generally unskilled workers.

Powered by two 1 980 lb (900 kg) thrust Junkers Jumo 004 B1 axial-flow gas turbines, the world's first production jet, with a speed of 540 mph (870 km/h), a climb rate of 4 000 ft/min (1 219 m/min) and a range of 600 miles (966 km), was considered a pilot's aeroplane. With four 30-mm Rheinmetall MK 108 cannon and 24 R4M Orkan (Hurricane) 55-mm folding-fin rockets, the Me 262 also set the standard for future fighter armament.

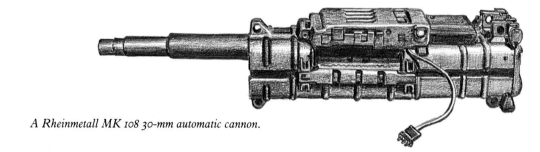

A Rheinmetall MK 108 30-mm automatic cannon.

Development of the Jet Engine

More than most developments, the jet engine changed the face of aviation. In Britain a true jet engine developed by Frank Whittle was bench-tested on 12 April 1937, and although it developed uncontrolled acceleration, it marked the beginning of Britain's long list of achievements in the field of gas turbine development.

The world's first jet aircraft, the Heinkel He 178, flew for the first time on 27 August 1939. Developed by Dr Hans-Joachim von Ohain, the 1 102 lb (496 kg) thrust turbojet with its 2-stage compressor and single-stage turbine was a neat, compact installation fitted into a fuselage not unlike that of the North American F-86 Sabre.

The Heinkel He 280 V-I – the first aircraft designed as a jet fighter – flew for the first time on 2 April 1941. Fitted with an ejection seat, this attractive, promising aircraft was dropped in favour of the Messerschmitt Me 262.

Britain's first experimental jet aircraft, the Gloster E 28/39, made its maiden flight on 15 May 1941. Just as the Heinkel He 280 evolved from the Heinkel He 178, the famous Gloster Meteor fighter was developed from the Gloster E 28/39. In Germany the Messerschmitt Me 262 made its first flight on 18 July 1942. This exceptionally advanced aircraft was, without doubt, the leading edge of aviation at the time.

Notes on the finish

When examined at Central Flying School Dunnottar in 1955, the fascinating, shark-like shape finished in bright green and brown mottle looked nothing like the standard soft Blue-Grey (RLM 76) with Purple Grey (RLM 75) mottle used for Luftwaffe nightfighters.

The upper flying surfaces were semi-gloss Light Green (RLM 83), and all undersides were matt Black. The fuselage and vertical tail surfaces had a field coat of RLM 76. A fine mottle of RLM 83 and Brown-Violet (RLM 81) were applied with a fascinating effect. Because RLM 83 contained a strong yellow constituent, it influenced the pale RLM 76 when air-brushed, creating a soft yellow effect around the green, while the RLM 81 took on a strong brown cast. The Black turbine nacelles had Green (RLM 82) upper surfaces forward of the leading edge.

The serial number 305 painted on the nose in White, and the White-outlined Red 8 roughly painted with a slight forward slope, were original markings. The insignia were overpainted in RAF Medium Sea Grey, as were the gunports. Originally the swastika (Hakenkreuz) was stencilled in Black. The fuselage Balkenkreuz was stencilled in Black outline only. On the undersides the Balkenkreuz was in White.

South Africa's Messerschmitt Me 262 (red 8 of Nachtjagdgeschwader 11) is portrayed as it was in 1955 while stored in Hangar 2 at Central Flying School, in the colours worn during the defence of Berlin ten years earlier.

Messerschmitt Me 262 B-1A/U-1 • 123

In bright sunshine above typical Transvaal afternoon storm clouds, a de Havilland Venom nears Swartkop Air Base.

De Havilland 112 Venom FB 1

In July 1955 three dots seemed to drop out of the Transvaal sky over Swartkop Air Base. Rapidly growing in size, they shrieked over the main runway at high speed, broke and landed with a banshee-like wail somewhat louder than that of the de Havilland Vampire. They turned out to be de Havilland 112 Venom FB 1s, and as in pre-war years, these beautifully maintained fighters had undertaken a goodwill visit, flying from the Middle East to the Cape.

The Venoms of 6 Squadron RAF were finished in a camouflage scheme, which contrasted sharply with the SAAF aircraft at the base finished in natural metal and Silver. Obviously developed from the Vampire, the Venom had a wing of a thinner section and with a swept leading edge. A 4 800 lb (2 160 kg) thrust DH Ghost 103 gas turbine engine gave the Venom a top speed of 640 mph (1 030 km/h), a rate of climb of 9 000 ft/min (2 743 m/min) and a ceiling in excess of 40 000 ft (12 192 m). All service Venoms were fitted with ejection seats.

Notes on the finish

The standard RAF fighter scheme of Dark Green and Dark Sea Grey in a disruptive pattern on the upper surfaces and Photo Reconnaissance Unit Blue undersides (all in high gloss) was well maintained. D-type roundels

Auster AOP 5

In 1955 Central Flying School Dunnottar saw a great deal of activity. Apart from the intense training program on North American Harvards, numbers of Auster AOP 5s and 6s stationed at the base were continually active. Early in 1945 42 Aerial Observation Post flight was formed in Italy and equipped with Austers, and this unit became 42 Squadron on their return to the Union after the war, where they retained their Auster 5s and received new Auster 6s. These types were replaced in the early 1960s by Cessna 185s.

Derived from the United States Taylorcraft built in the United Kingdom, the Austers were operated in large numbers by the British Army during World War II. The Auster 5 was identical to the Mk 4, except for a blind-flying panel, and was powered by a Lycoming O-290 engine. The Mk 6 was fitted with a 145 hp (108 kW) de Havilland Gipsy Major 7 engine, and was designed with auxiliary flaps aft of the trailing edge, as well as a lengthened undercarriage.

Notes on the finish
Most of these aircraft seem to have been finished in Dark Earth overall, including the undersides of the fuselage. The undersides of the wings and tailplane were a Sky Blue which varied from FS 35190 to a paler FS 35177. Apparently patches of Green were later applied to the upper surfaces. Auster No 5404 wore this basic scheme, with the code OP-E painted in Yellow. It also had a Dark Green door, while from the rear of the cockpit (including the vertical tail surfaces), the fuselage was painted in a non-standard Medium Green resembling FS 34098. No insignia or serial numbers appeared on the wings, although prominent fuselage Springbok roundels were worn, as were fin flashes.

A Martin-Baker 2 ejection seat as fitted to the de Havilland Venom FB 1.

were applied to all surfaces. Venom WK404 wore its individual letter X (repeated in Red on the nosewheel door) behind the serial number. Squadron markings were used instead of code letters, and 6 Squadron's insignia was two Azure rectangles on either side of the boom roundel, outlined with BS Aircraft Blue and containing a Red chevron pattern. A decal of the official squadron badge, including the rectangles, was applied to the fuselage below the windscreen side panels. Above this was painted a small ace of hearts playing card emblem.

An Auster AOP 5 near Central Flying School Dunnottar in 1955.

Lockheed PV-1 Ventura

A Lockheed PV-1 Ventura circling the British troopship Empire Orwell as she nears the Cape Town dock entrance during the Suez Crisis of 1956. The ship was formerly the Deutsche Ost-Afrika Linie liner Pretoria (see p 26).

During the 1950s PV-1 Venturas were active along the coast as the standard in-shore maritime reconnaissance aircraft operated by 17 and 22 Squadrons based at Ysterplaat, until they were finally retired in 1960. Well-maintained and hard-worked, they were a credit to the SAAF, who managed to get the most out of their Venturas, which were unique in military aviation.

Notes on the finish

The standard finish of Extra Dark Sea Grey upper surfaces and Sky undersides included some interesting variations. One or two machines had Dark Sea Grey upper surfaces, and at least four aircraft displayed undersides slightly darker than Sky, with a brown cast – very much like FS 30372. Ventura L, 6515

(MT) was one of these. Another had FS 34258 undersides, which incidentally was also found on the undersides of a B-34 Ventura disposed of after the war. The squadron codes (MS for 17 Squadron and MT for 22 Squadron), were in Yellow, and individual aircraft letters were repeated, also in Yellow, on the tailplane above the rear fuselage. A Blue separating tape was used on the White nose radomes. Spinners and wheel covers were Red or Blue, depending on the flight, while the underside serial numbers were placed parallel to the wing leading edges.

Banking steeply, a Ventura passes the RMMV Capetown Castle — *perhaps the most beautifully proportioned ship of the Union Castle Line.*

Hawker Seahawk and de Havilland 112 Sea Venom

After a thirteen-month cruise to the Middle and Far East, HMS *Albion* paid a brief visit to Port Elizabeth during 1959 while on her way home. On board were 804 Squadron equipped with Hawker Seahawk FGA 6s, 809 Squadron with de Havilland Sea Venom FAW 21s, and a flight of Douglas Skyraider AEW 1s. Many of these aircraft took part in a fly-past over the city.

Although not the first jet fighter to join the Fleet Air Arm – that honour went to the Supermarine Attacker – the Seahawk seemed the logical replacement for the Hawker Sea Fury. Originally conceived as a fighter for the RAF, the Hawker P 1040, as it was known, first flew in 1947. After successful deck-handling trials, the Seahawk was adopted as the standard FAA fighter, entering service in 1953. The Seahawk went through many stages of development, from the F1, F2 and FB3 to the FGA 4, from which evolved the FGA 5 and 6 versions with their uprated power plants.

The Seahawk FGA 6s of 800, 802, 804, 897 and 899 Squadrons acquitted themselves well during the Anglo-French invasion of Egypt during the 1956 Suez crisis, carrying out many ground-attack sorties against Egyptian airfields. These popular aircraft were replaced by the Supermarine Scimitar (the last aircraft from that famous stable) in 1960.

Powered by the 5 400 lb (2 450 kg) thrust Rolls-Royce Nene 103 centrifugal turbine engine, a maximum speed of 630 mph (1 014 km/h), a climb rate of 9 000 ft/min (2 743 m/min) and a range of 1 400 miles (2 253 km) with drop tanks was attained. The underwing load comprised ten rockets and two 500-lb

Passing over Cape Recife in 1959, a Hawker Seahawk and de Havilland Sea Venom from HMS Albion prepare to form up with other aircraft to fly over Port Elizabeth.

(227 kg) bombs in addition to the standard four 20-mm cannon.

The Sea Venom had the same flying surfaces as the RAF Venom fighters, but the fuselage, redesigned to accommodate a pilot and observer, had a side-by-side cockpit reminiscent of the Mosquito and Vampire T 55. The Sea Venom FAW 21, with its large nose radome, was an all-weather and strike fighter, and also saw action during the Suez crisis, operating alongside Seahawks.

With a 4 950 lb (2 245 kg) thrust de Havilland Ghost 104 centrifugal turbine engine, a speed of 620 mph (998 km/h), climb rate of 8 762 ft/min (2 670 m/min) and range of 1 000 miles (1 600 km) was achieved, which compared very well with the Seahawk. In addition to a fixed armament of four 20-mm cannon, eight rockets or bombs could be carried. In 1960 the Sea Venom was succeeded by the de Havilland 110 Sea Vixen.

Notes on the finish
The Seahawks of HMS *Albion* were finished in the latest fighter scheme of gloss Extra Dark Sea Grey upper surfaces and Off-White undersides. With a very slight cream tint the 'broken white' differed slightly from the roundel colour. In contrast to when Sky was the standard underside finish, the fin and rudder were treated as upper surfaces. D-type roundels were worn on all surfaces, but, as usual, no fin flashes were applied. The carrier code letter A was painted on the fin in Black, and the aircraft number forward of the intake. The 804 Squadron insignia (a Black and White tiger's head) was painted on the nose.

In contrast the Sea Venom was finished in the earlier scheme of Extra Dark Sea Grey with Sky undersides (including the fin and rudder), and appeared very colourful as a result of graphics which had reached their limit as far as British aircraft were concerned. Apart from the standard insignia and aircraft number, the upper section of each rudder was painted Red, with the ship's code letter A in White. Wingtip tanks were Black with White cheat lines and fins, while the squadron insignia (a Red Griffon) was painted on the fuselage ahead of the aircraft number.

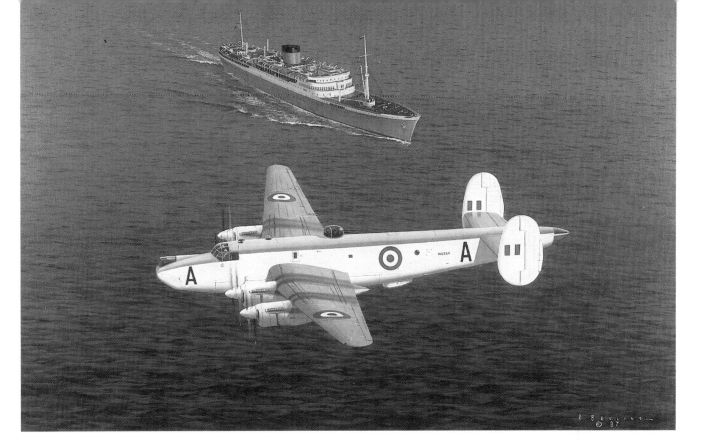

Avro Shackleton 2

In 1953 a distinctive sound was heard in South African skies for the first time. Passengers aboard RMMV *Capetown Castle*, on a coastal voyage, were impressed by a large, attractive aircraft that circled the ship, its four Rolls-Royce Griffon engines reverberating with a two-tone musical crescendo which receded into a droning throb as the Avro Shackleton 2 flew off towards Durban like a graceful white and grey seabird.

Those with an experienced eye could discern the machine's lineage: it had the lengthened Lancaster wings adopted for the Lincoln, and these, together with a new, more spacious fuselage, made the Shackleton 1. It was found, however, that the chin radome on this particular mark was susceptible to bird strikes, so a new nose was designed and the radome installed as a dustbin amidships. Thus the Shackleton 2 was born.

42 Squadron, RAF, was the first to be equipped with Shackleton 2s, which were flown to South Africa on a goodwill tour to demonstrate them to the SAAF, which at the time was planning to replace its ageing Short Sunderlands. In June 1955 204 Squadron visited these shores, also with Shackleton 2s. As a result an order for eight Shackleton 3s was placed to re-equip 35 Squadron of the SAAF. Improved sound insulation as well as revised wings with wingtip tanks and a tricycle undercarriage made the Shackleton 3 a more efficient machine, but also eliminated all visible links with the original Manchester/Lancaster concept.

Notes on the finish
The Shackleton was finished in the standard RAF Maritime Reconnaissance finish of Medium Sea Grey upper surfaces, gloss White undersides and matt White fuselage flanks and vertical tail surfaces, with D-type roundels on the upper wing surfaces and fuselage. The fuselage squadron codes and serial numbers were in Black.

During a goodwill tour of South Africa in 1953 this Avro Shackleton 2 gracefully banks over the RMMV Capetown Castle *near Durban, a powerful note emanating from its Rolls Royce Griffon engines.*

Avro Shackleton 3

At about 21h00 on 18 April 1958 a strange aircraft circled Port Elizabeth. The reverberating drone of the powerful engines changed to a whining crackle as the machine passed low over Walmer on its landing approach. The following morning, a new SAAF Avro Shackleton 3 (No 1722, P) was seen parked on the main airport apron, looking attractive in its new gloss paintwork.

Initially fitted with eight underwing zero-length rocket launchers for a limited strike capability, the Shackletons were also equipped for air-sea rescue duties. Shackleton No 1717 (O), fitted with a Saro 3 airborne lifeboat, was stationed in Port Elizabeth for a few days in July 1960, while acting as a standby during one of 35 Squadron's long-range undertakings.

Operating from D F Malan airport in Cape Town, and with maintenance facilities at Ysterplaat, 35 Squadron undertook long-range patrols along the South African coastline. When passing Port Elizabeth, they invariably carried out a low-level beat-up of the main runway at the Air Base. No flying activity viewed from the ground could be more exhilarating in sound and sight. The large, glossy Blue and Grey aircraft with their four engines thundered only a few feet above the runway, their counter-rotating propellers forming clear arcs and the wing-tip tanks tending to increase the long-span dihedral. As they gracefully pulled up, the engine note changed to the familiar drone, dominated by a receding whining crackle.

Apart from the accidental loss of No 1718 (K) on 8 August 1963, the Shackletons established a proud record of reliability, their electronic equipment being updated whenever possible. Among their many tasks where the monitoring of the movements of Soviet warships rounding the Cape, which often had its surprises. After 27 years' service, No 1716 (J) was the last recorded out of Port Elizabeth. When it took off at dusk on 4 October 1984, the beat-up sounded all the more dramatic in the clear calm of the early evening.

Powered by four 2 450 hp (1 830 kW) Rolls-Royce Griffon 57 engines, the Shackleton 3 attained a maximum speed of 302 mph (486 km/h), a climb rate of 850 ft/min (259 m/min), a ceiling of 19 200 ft (5 852 m) and a range of 4 215 miles (6 783 km) at a maximum weight of 100 000 lb (45 455 kg) — some 14 000 lb (6 364 kg) heavier than the Shackleton 2.

Notes on the finish
When delivered, the Shackletons had BS gloss Extra Dark Sea Grey upper surfaces and gloss Photo Reconnaissance Unit Blue undersides, fuselage flanks and vertical tail surfaces as well as a Yellow aircraft letter forward of the fuselage insignia. A fairly large Black serial number on the rear fuselage was repeated on the undersides. Although delivered in Springbok roundels, these very soon gave way to Castle insignia. Fin flashes were painted on outer vertical surfaces and the wing walkway lines were Yellow.

It was found necessary to apply matt Black anti-glare panels to the fuselage forward of the cockpit and White fuselage decking. Because the White lined up with the tailplane centreline, a strip of the original Extra Dark Sea Grey initially separated the White from the PRU Blue. This was later eliminated when the aircraft underwent repainting. During the 1970s the front sections of the spinners were painted Red — a practice retained until their retirement.

A Shackleton 3 (shown shortly after delivery) passing over USS Essex *in 1957. Note the Springbok roundels, which were later replaced by Castle insignia.*

An Avro Shackleton 3 on patrol over a stormy Algoa Bay in 1960. The trawler Jack is typical of a class that served along the coast.

Douglas Skyraider AEW-1 and AD-4N

Right: *A Douglas Skyraider AEW-1 flies along the Algoa Bay coastline while HMS Albion makes way.*

Below: *A Skyraider AD-4N of the French Armée de l'Air over the tropical coastline of Madagascar.*

While HMS *Albion* cruised in Algoa Bay to pick up her aircraft, the dark guppy shape of a lone Douglas Skyraider AEW-1 was accompanied by the slow, deep throbbing rumble of its powerful engine as it flew along the shoreline. Attached to 'C' Flight of 849 Squadron, it was one of the carrier-borne radar pickets of the Fleet Air Arm. Delivered from the United States, these aircraft fulfilled the important role of air early warning by carrying nearly a ton of powerful radar equipment, with the scanner housed in an enormous fibreglass ventral guppy radome.

With the outbreak of war in Korea, Skyraiders made a major contribution to ending that conflict, as they did later during the Vietnam struggle. The AD-4W was supplied to the Royal Navy in 1951 under the Mutual Defence Assistance Programme, where it was given the British designation AEW-1. Until replaced in 1960 by the Fairey Gannet AEW-3, it proved an excellent aircraft, being seen in action against Egypt during the 1956 Suez Crisis.

In 1959 the French Armée de l'Air received more than a hundred surplus US Navy Skyraider AD-4Ns for extensive counter-insurgency operations in the African colonies of Algeria, Somaliland and Madagascar. In October 1973 four Skyraiders of Escadron d'Appui Aérien 2/21, Madagascar, were on deck aboard the *Argens* when she docked in Port Elizabeth on her way to France. They were fitted with additional external armour-plating, as was found on the Douglas AD-6 and AD-7 Skyraider. One of the US Navy's most successful aircraft, the Skyraider was used in a multitude of roles until its retirement from that service in 1968.

Originally designed to meet a World War II requirement for a replacement for the Dauntless dive bomber, the Douglas XBT-2 D-1, initially named the Dauntless II, was the first single-seat carrier-based dive and torpedo bomber. It was finally designated the AD-1 Skyraider, but appeared too late to take an active part in World War II. The AD-2, 3 and 4 were development stages of this type. The AD-4 was a single-seat strike aircraft with effective dive brakes, the AD-4N was designed for night operations and the AD-4W was equipped with early warning radar. Both the N and the W variant had a small door with a circular window for access to the electronics operator's station.

Powered by a 2 700 hp Wright R-3350 engine, the Skyraider AD-4 carried an external load of 8 000 lb (3 636 kg) and had a fixed armament of 4 20-mm cannon. A maximum speed of 318 mph (512 km/h), an initial climb rate of 2 380 ft/min (725 m/min), a service ceiling of 32 000 ft (9 754 m) and a range of 900 miles (1 448 km) were attained.

Notes on the finish

The Skyraider AEW-1s of the FAA were finished in overall gloss Sea Blue (FS 15042) and wore D-type roundels in all positions. The carrier code letter on the fin, the flight letter on the nose and the aircraft number aft of the fuselage roundel were all in White. Skyraider WT959 (424) was formerly a United States machine (No 127957).

French Skyraider AD-4Ns were Silver overall, with Black letters, numbers, antiglare panels and side panels. The rudder tops, wingtips and fronts of the undercarriage covers where Red, with the aircraft letter in White on the rudder top. Skyraider No 21-ZH carried its United States Bu number (126970) in Black on the lower fin area (see detail below). Standard French Air Force roundels were worn on all surfaces, but no fin flashes were applied. Where the Silver paint had peeled, the original US Sea Blue was revealed. The other three machines were Nos 21-ZI (Bu No 126949), 21-ZD (Bu No 126922) and 21-ZG (Bu No 126882).

The last sunlight of dusk touches the higher clouds as a Lockheed PV-1 Ventura with undercarriage and flaps down lines up with the main runway of the Port Elizabeth Airport in December 1959.

Lockheed PV-1 Ventura

On 4 December 1959 one of four Lockheed PV-1 Venturas on an exercise flight from Cape Town to Port Elizabeth experienced an engine failure near Mossel Bay. By the time the aircraft arrived over the Port Elizabeth Air Base, a south-westerly gale had blown up, so the pilot of the stricken aircraft elected to go round rather than coming straight in with the strong tailwind. While banking, however, the Ventura rolled over out of control, crashed and exploded near a residential area.

The following day the crash enquiry team arrived aboard a VIP Ventura (No 6462). While starting up for the return flight, one of its engines burst into flames. Fitted with a new engine, the aircraft was on its way to Pretoria via Durban a week later, but another powerplant problem developed. Unfortunately it ended up in a dry riverbed near Port St Johns, but luckily none of the seven people on board were killed. But the writing was on the wall for the venerable Ventura: even the SAAF could not keep them going any longer, so they were taken out of service.

Notes on the finish

Before they ended their service, a number of PV-1 Venturas wore a finish which was in line with the new Maritime Reconnaissance finish introduced on the SAAF's Avro Shackletons. One of the Venturas (No 6472) wore an upper surface finish of Dark Sea Grey which, incidentally, matched the upper surface finish of the SAAF's Hawker-Siddeley Buccaneers, not the Extra Dark Sea Grey of the Shackletons. The undersides were finished in Photo Reconnaissance Unit Blue with a single Yellow aircraft letter (in this case D) which was placed immediately ahead of the Castle insignia. All the paintwork was gloss.

North American Mustang, the North American XP-86 Fury – with flying surfaces very much like those of the Mustang – was expected to have a maximum speed of 580 mph (933 km/h). However, when details of the Messerschmitt Me 262 and the wing design of the Messerschmitt Me P1101 became known and test data was made available, the project underwent a redesign. Now with swept wings and tail surfaces, the North American F-86 Sabre was to become the West's first supersonic fighter. In 1949 it joined the US Air Force as the world's most advanced fighter, and went on to establish an outstanding record during the Korean conflict, where it was also flown by 2 Squadron of the SAAF – The Flying Cheetahs.

The Sabre was also constructed in Canada under licence with the designation Canadair CL-13, and this was the source from which the SAAF purchased their aircraft. Thirty-four CL-13B 6s, powered by the 7 275 lb (3 300 kg) thrust Avro Orenda 14 turbojet engine, were delivered to 1 and 2 Squadrons. The Sabre 6 attained 710 mph (1 143 km/h) at sea level, 620 mph (998 km/h) at 36 000 ft (10 973 m), and initially climbed at 11 800 ft/min (3 597 m/min) to a ceiling of 50 000 ft (15 240 m). The range of 800 miles (1 287 km) could be extended to 1 485 miles (2 390 km) with long-range tanks.

In 1963 the Mirage IIICZ began replacing the Sabres of 2 Squadron, but they served as operation trainers until retired in 1980.

Canadair CL-13B Sabre 6

A Canadair Sabre 6 performs a low-level beat-up of the Port Elizabeth Airport in July 1959, and the late afternoon sun reflects off the metal finish as it tears over the runway.

When the first five Canadair Sabre 6s from 2 Squadron arrived in Port Elizabeth in July 1959 with a thunderous roar from their axial-flow turbines and a flash of their swept flying surfaces, these remarkable machines dramatically displayed the developments that had taken place in the field of high-speed technology, begun in Germany more than twenty years earlier.

The two SAAF units equipped with these aircraft regularly flew to Port Elizabeth on training exercises. Usually arriving before lunch, they independently took off for Waterkloof at dusk. Before heading north, each aircraft would carry out a low-level beat-up of the Air Base. Coming in low, trailing smoke, but with no sound, their tail fins like that of a shark, their underslung tanks almost touching the runway, they would streak past with a tearing, thunderlike sound which roared and crackled through the evening calm.

Originally conceived as a jet version of the

Notes on the finish

Due to variations in alloys and construction techniques, the panels of the natural metal finish differed in colour. 2 Squadron had BS Post Office Red diagonal fuselage bands, wing tips and cheat lines on their long-range tanks. A thin Black outline was applied to the Red trim, except on the fuel tanks. The stylized fin flashes effectively related to the vertical tail shape. Each machine wore a Red identification letter ahead of the fuselage Castle. 1 Squadron had the same markings, but these were painted in Aircraft Blue outlined with Orange. Initially their long-range tanks had Blue and Orange bands instead of cheat lines. Both units had small versions of their insignia painted below the cockpits.

Sikorsky S-55 and S-58

When the dock landing ship USS *Donner* (LSD-20) tied up in Port Elizabeth in October 1961, two US Navy helicopters from Utility Squadron HU-4 were on board.

Igor Sikorsky was one of the world leaders in helicopter design, and built the R-4, which was the first Allied helicopter to enter service. His next design was the R-5 (redesignated S-51 Dragonfly – see p 120), and this was the first helicopter type to serve with the SAAF. In United States service it was followed by the S-55, which was referred to in the US Navy as the HO4 in its general-purpose and anti-submarine observation role and the HRS in its transport role, in which it was capable of carrying eight troops and a pilot. The HRS-2 aboard *Donner* was fitted with a 550 hp (410 kW) Pratt & Whitney R-1430 engine, which gave it a maximum speed of 101 mph (163 km/h) and a range of 370 miles (595 km).

The S-58 was designed to show an improvement over the limited load capacity of the S-55, and was known as the HSS Seabat and used for naval anti-submarine duties. The marine equivalent used for transport was the HUS-1 Seahorse, which could carry a crew of two and between 12 and 18 passengers. With a 1 525 hp (1 140 kW) Wright R-1820 engine, a speed of 123 mph (198 km/h) and a range of 182 miles (293 km) was attained.

Notes on the finish
The HRS-2 (S-55) was finished in a bright overall scheme of Fluorescent Yellow-Orange (FS 28915), but the paint had become slightly faded on the upper surfaces due to the effects of ultra-violet and salt air. It wore an unusual White surround to the national insignia and an incomplete representation of the globe on the nose.

An overall finish of Field Green (FS 34097) on the HUS-1 (S-58) incorporated nose and tail panels in FS 28915. All lettering was White and the badge on the nose comprised an FS 35190 background with land masses in FS 34097, the ribbon in FS 35109 and the letter A in Yellow. The US flags on both machines were unusual in that the Blue was painted in FS 35190.

A Sikorsky HRS-2 (S-55) comes in to touch down on USS Donner *while at sea off Algoa Bay in 1961. A Sikorsky HUS-1 (S-58) is parked on the deck.*

Dornier Do 27

In 1959 the capabilities of a civil Dornier Do 27 (D-EMAM) were demonstrated by Heinz Schaefer (well-known for his outstanding displays at the annual Farnborough Air Show) when he performed almost every possible manoeuvre apart from hovering over the Port Elizabeth Air Base. Another example of the type was seen there when a SAAF machine (No 5430) spent a few days at Eastern Province Command in January 1962.

Developed from the Dornier Do 25, the first post-war machine to bear the company's name, the Do 27 was a light transport with short take-off and landing (STOL) capabilities likened to the Fieseler Storch which served with the Luftwaffe during World War II. The SAAF bought two Do 27s as trial machines when it was found necessary to replace their Austers, but no further Dorniers were ordered. Cessna 185s were bought instead.

Notes on the finish
On delivery both machines were finished in natural metal, but they soon received a finish of matt Dark Earth upper surfaces and Photo Reconnaissance Unit Blue undersides. The latter colour seemed slightly paler with a more grey cast than the BS Blue. Castle insignia were applied to all surfaces, and as usual the Black serial number was repeated on the underside. The spinner and propeller were in natural metal with Yellow tips. The cockpit was beautifully padded in off-white

Hedge-hopping in the Bathurst district near Grahamstown, this Dornier Do 27 almost becomes part of the rolling landscape.

Lockheed P2V-5F Neptune

On 9 August 1963 an RAF Shackleton 3 from 120 Squadron landed at the Port Elizabeth Airport, and shortly after a second aircraft came into view. With props and jets running, it made a low pass over the main runway and disappeared in a westerly direction. The aircraft turned out to be a US Navy Lockheed Neptune, one of two from VP-16 to take part in combined operations involving the SAAF, RAF, French Aéronavale and US Navy.

The two aircraft that appeared over Port Elizabeth were, however, taking part in a real search for SAAF Shackleton No 1718 which had dissapeared while on a mission. It had been due to intercept shipping off Algoa Bay, so the search included the coast in that area.

The Neptune, a rare type along the Republic's coast, was the successor to the famous Lockheed line which included the Hudson, B-34 and PV-1 Ventura and PV-2 Harpoon. Built in seven models, this very successful aircraft served with the US Navy from 1947 until replaced by the Lockheed P-3 Orion. Kawasaki in Japan built the P2V-KAI, a P-2J with turboprops. Powered by two 3 750 hp (2 800 kW) Wright Cyclone R-3350 engines and two 3 240 lb (1 470 kg) thrust Westinghouse J34 turbojets, the P2V-5 attained a maximum speed of 323 mph (520 km/h) and a range of 4 750 miles (7 644 km). An ordnance load of 10 000 lb (4 500 kg) could be carried.

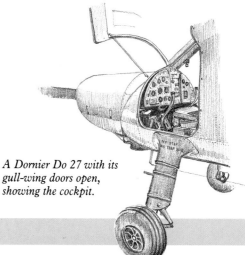

A Dornier Do 27 with its gull-wing doors open, showing the cockpit.

R BELLINC © 87

Notes on the finish

The RAF Shackleton was finished in gloss Dark Sea Grey overall with White fuselage decking, its RAF lettering in White and the serial number XF704 in Red. The number 120 at mid-fuselage, the individual aircraft letter D on the nose and the underwing serial number were in Red, outlined in White. Small D-type roundels were positioned above the wing trailing edge.

Apart from the gloss insignia, White fuselage decking and tail, the Neptune was finished in Seaplane Gray (FS 26081). The only difference between this and Engine Gray (FS 16081) is that the former is a semi-gloss finish whereas FS 16081 is glossy. All lettering was White. The squadron code (LF) was repeated on the upper starboard surface and the word 'Navy' appeared on the lower.

In company over Cape Recife, a US Navy Lockheed Neptune and an RAF Avro Shackleton 3 share a patrol during Operation Capex in 1963.

Pulling up shortly after take-off in May 1963, this Lockheed Hercules is shown against a background of southern storm clouds reflecting a late afternoon sun.

Lockheed C-130B Hercules

As the first SAAF Lockheed C-130B Hercules (No 402) to visit Port Elizabeth taxied to its parking area in May 1963, the deep and powerful yet soft rumble of its four 4 050 shp (3 030 kW) Allison T-56 turboprop engines changed to a persistent soft whine. From then onwards this has been a sound heard almost daily at SAAF bases, as well as at civil airports, as the SAAF ordered seven Hercules for general transport, paratrooping and air search purposes.

The aircraft has a well-designed fuselage with a sharply tapered rear underside to accommodate a ramp for the easy loading of heavy cargo. Capable of carrying a payload of 25 000 lb (11 250 kg) at a speed of 375 mph (604 km/h) over a range of 3 400 miles (5 472 km) with a ceiling of 30 000 ft (9 144 m) at a gross weight of 135 000 lb (61 240 kg), the Hercules is 35 per cent heavier than the Shackleton 3. Operated by 28 Squadron, the Hercules has rendered excellent service on countless operational flights.

Notes on the finish

On delivery the natural metal finish of the Hercules was well polished and the gloss White fuselage decking was separated by a thin Blue stripe which neatly surrounded the upper section of the fuselage Castle insignia, while the words SA Lugmag/SA Air Force had been painted in Blue behind the cockpit. Panels between the spars above and below the mainplane, as well as the walkway on the fuselage decking were painted in Aircraft Grey (FS 16473). The serial numbers (402) on the nose, fin and undersides were in gloss Black, while the radome, spinners and propeller de-icers were in matt Black. All Blue, which should have been BS Aircraft Blue, was US Insignia Blue (FS 15044) instead, and in the place of Flag Orange in the fin flash, International Orange (FS 12197) was used.

Westland Wasp

SAS *Simon van der Stel* carried out her maiden cruise as a re-built helicopter-carrying submarine hunter during October 1964. Originally HMS *Whelp*, she had lost some of her sleekness due to the removal of her forward gun turret and the addition of a box-like hangar, but the raked funnel and bow left her with some of the appearance of the greyhound she had been.

Shortly before docking in Port Elizabeth during this cruise, her two Westland Wasp helicopters flew over the city. Delivered in 1964, they equipped the newly-established 22 Flight. Powered by a gas turbine engine, the Wasp is said to be the first helicopter designed to operate from small ships in rought seas. The fully-castering undercarriage could effectively absorb heavy landings, and the folding rotor blades and tail unit allowed stowage in small hangars.

Powered by a 710 shp (530 kW) Rolls-Royce/Bristol Nimbus shaft turbine, the Wasp attained a maximum speed of 120 mph (193 km/h), had a range of 270 miles (435 km) and carried the effective armament of two homing torpedoes, two depth charges or an assortment of missiles. At the time the Wasp was a potent anti-submarine weapon.

Notes on the finish

Wasps Nos 82 and 84 served aboard SAS *Simon van der Stel*. No 84 was finished in what became the standard colour of gloss Dark Sea Grey, with White lettering. On the other hand No 82 was finished in gloss Photo Reconnaissance Unit Blue overall, possibly as a test colour. It also had White lettering, but the Castle insignia had Orange springboks in place of the standard Gold. The flotation balls were dull Yellow and deep Blue-Green. After ditching in 1967, No 82 was salvaged and rebuilt, and re-entered service with a Dark Sea Grey finish.

Two Westland Wasps circle SAS Simon van der Stel *as she slices through a calm sea in Algoa Bay.*

Dassault Mirage IIICZ

The first Mirage IIICZs visited Port Elizabeth on 7 January 1965. With the thunderous, penetrating roar of their SNECMA-Atar turbojets, their arrow-shaped wings, remarkable speed and climbing ability, they thrilled the crowds gathered at the airport that afternoon to see one of the machines being put through its paces.

When the SAAF took delivery of their first Mirages in 1963, they took on charge one of the most advanced fighters of the time. Apart from the CZ version, the SAAF put into service Mirage IIIBZ, DZ, EZ and RZ versions between 1964 and 1968. These were followed by the swept-wing F1AZ and F1CZ in the 1970s and the Atlas Cheetah during the 1980s. Presently the Mirage family (which the SAAF are exploiting to the maximum with their usual skill) has been superseded by later generations of aircraft in the international warplane arena. However, on the occasions that SAAF Mirages have had to fire their guns in anger, they have aquitted themselves well.

An interesting aspect of the Mirage evolution which is not fully recognized is that it represents the culmination of three German systems conceived and under development during World War II. To its credit the French aircraft industry recognized their potential, perfected them and turned them into winners.

Alexander Lippisch was a glider designer with the Deutsches Forschungsinstitut für Segelflug (German Glider Research Institute) and was later employed by Messerschmitt to design the radical Me 163 Komet rocket fighter. His research led him to conceive the delta-wing as a simple answer to high-speed flight, and in 1942 he also took the first patent for variable swept wings. After the war Lippisch worked as consultant to Convair, and this firm perfected the F-102 Delta Dagger and F-106 Delta Dart fighters. During this period low-speed stability problems were partially resolved by the introduction of a cambered wing leading edge, and the Mirage wing followed this principle.

In 1943 Mauser built the most advanced aircraft cannon of the war, the 20-mm MG 213C and its 30-mm derivative the MK 213C. By the time the Allies overran Germany, the weapon was perfected and about to go into production. Tests had shown that a high rate of fire and muzzle velocity as well as a long barrel life were possible due to a special bore polishing process, and the concept was adopted by the United States, Britain, France, Switzerland and Russia. In the RAF it became known as the Aden and in the Armée de l'Air as the Defa (the model used in the Mirage and Impala 2).

During World War II the BMW 003 axial-flow turbojet had gone into production, but

already second-generation powerplants were under development. The BMW 018 turbojet and 028 turboprop were nearly ready for testing when the war ended. The BMW design team under Dr H. Oestrich established themselves in Rickenbach, Switzerland, to continue the development under the name Atelier Technique Aeronautique Rickenbach (Atar). At the end of 1945 the French Government awarded a development contract for the Atar, provided that it was built in France. SNECMA, a new company building German Argus-derived in-line Renault 12S engines (see p 116) were selected to build the turbojet. Later the German team were absorbed by SNECMA, with Oestrich as technical director. Soon after the SNECMA-Atar 101V, the first French gas turbine, was born.

Powered by the SNECMA-Atar 9 of between 13 225 lb and 15 000 lb (6 000 and 6 800 kg) thrust, the Mirage III attained a speed of 863 mph (1 388 km/h) at sea level and 1 460 mph (2 350 km/h) at altitude. Climbing at 16 400 ft/min (5 000 m/min) to a ceiling of 55 000 ft (16 764 m), it had a range of 1 000 miles (1 600 km) or 2 485 miles (4 000 km) with external fuel tanks.

Notes on the finish
On delivery from France the Mirages were finished in natural metal with an assortment of hues due to variations in the alloys. Mirage No 813 was a typical example, with the trim around the intakes and behind the cockpit, the lightning flash along the fuselage and the aircraft letter (P in this case) on the fin painted in BS Post Office Red. As it was a 2 Squadron aircraft, the flying cheetah insignia in the newly-introduced circular design with a black background was applied to the upper fin. Of interest is the national insignia, which used the French Insignia Blue, but were duly repainted with SAAF Blue.

Later SAAF Mirages were camouflaged in gloss Deep Buff, Olive Drab and Light Admirality Grey. A matt finish was later found more effective, and at present low-visibility schemes are being introduced. In practice these have been found to be a great improvement over the Deep Buff, which shows up very brightly at altitude.

Douglas B-26C Invader

During 1966 an elegant aircraft whose engines made the same deep rumble as the Lockheed Ventura was regularly seen in South African skies while carrying out a geological survey, and in September this Douglas B-26C Invader spent a few days in Port Elizabeth. Operated by a French company, the machine was still in its basic operational finish and had obviously not long previously been serving in the French Armée de l'Air.

In 1941 Douglas introduced the A-26 as a successor to the A-20 Boston. Known as the Invader, it was built as the A-26B fighter (with solid nose) and the A-26C, with a fully-glazed forward section for light bombardment duties. Although bearing a strong family resemblance to the Boston, the B-26 (to use its later designation) was more angular, with slender wings and fuselage. The engines were housed in two enormous nacelles attractively extended well behind the wing trailing edge.

The Armée de l'Air bought a number, which served in French Indo-China, and when the United States became embroiled in

the struggle they too operated the B-26 (the B-26K, which had strengthened wings, wingtip tanks and square-tipped propellers). After their withdrawal from Indo-China the French operated B-26Cs over Algeria, from where they were retired in the mid-1960s.

Fitted with 2 000 hp (1 500 kW) Pratt & Whitney R-2800 engines, the Invader had a maximum speed of 373 mph (600 km/h), a ceiling of 22 850 ft (6 965 m), a bomb load of 4 000 lb (1 800 kg) and a range of 1 400 miles (2 253 km).

Notes on the finish
The Invader was painted in its combat finish of overall matt Black with White fuselage decking, and wore the civil registration F-BMKT in White on the fin and rudder. All military markings were overpainted Black. From behind the gills the engine nacelles were heavily streaked by pale grey exhaust oxidation and oil.

Climbing over the Swartkops River, the matt Black finish of this Douglas Invader stands in stark contrast to the glow of the golden early-morning sun.

A Hawker-Siddeley Buccaneer over Port Elizabeth in June 1966, with the port, central city, airport and Algoa Bay in the foreground, and the Indian Ocean behind.

Hawker-Siddeley Buccaneer S 50

On 17 June 1966 Buccaneers Nos 413 and 419 flew down to Port Elizabeth to take part in a successful air display. No 419 put on an outstanding performance, making tight turns to the accompaniment of the thunderous tone of its twin turbines.

Blackburn (later Hawker-Siddeley) mainly built naval aircraft and designed the Buccaneer as a land- and carrier-based low-level attack aircraft capable of penetrating radar screens by flying at near transonic speed 'on the deck' with outstanding stability and comfort. Capable of carrying nuclear stores, the type could be operated as a stand-off bomber, lobbing its bombs while climbing from low level and banking so that it is on its way back when the bombs hit their target.

Compared to the dart-like Mirage, the hefty Buccaneer with its loaded weight in excess of 30 tons is certainly a large aircraft. It is also an attractive aircraft, but its profile and contours have the appearance of an insect with a large tail sting – especially when viewed from the rear.

With two Rolls-Royce Spey 101 turbofans developing 11 030 lbs (4 964 kg) thrust each at sea level, a speed of Mach .85, an initial climb rate of 7 000 ft/min (2134 m/min), a ceiling of 40 000 ft (12 192 m), a total armaments load of 16 000 lb (7 200 kg) and a range of 2 300 miles (3 701 km) are attained.

Notes on the finish

On delivery the Buccaneers were finished with gloss Dark Sea Grey upper surfaces and Photo Reconnaissance Unit Blue undersides. The two colours are almost the same shade, whereas there is a noticeable difference between the Shackleton's Extra Dark Sea Grey and PRU Blue. There were a matt Black anti-glare panel and area under the rear fuselage, and Castle insignia were worn forward of the intakes, and the 24 Squadron crest on the sides. Up to the mainplane and intakes the leading edges were left in natural metal, while the fibreglass nose radome was painted with a yellow gold colour. At a later stage the gloss finish was replaced by matt, and the radome, anti-glare panel and fin flashes overpainted to match the overall scheme, while the size of the Castle insignia was reduced.

In accordance with the Simon's Town Agreement concluded between Britain and South Africa, the latter country was required to have on strength a long-range low-level attack aircraft. As a result 16 Hawker-Siddeley Buccaneer S 50s were ordered and in 1965 24 Squadron was reformed at Waterkloof. The S 50 version was almost identical to the British Buccaneer 2, but had provision for a rocket pack to assist with emergency take-offs from high-level airfields, especially in Africa.

Because of the type of operations undertaken by the aircraft, the attrition rate has been high, but in spite of this 24 Squadron is still very active with its brutes. The residents of Waterkloof are often reminded of this when the Buccaneers take off on pre-dawn exercises with a thundering roar.

English Electric Canberra B 2

The English Electric Canberra was Britain's first jet bomber, and made its public debut at the 1949 Farnborough Air Show. It surprised spectators by the remarkable ease with which it was thrown about, like a fighter. It had a cigar-shaped fuselage, slender nacelles housing axial-flow turbojets and conventional low aspect-ratio wings. As was the case with the de Havilland Mosquito, defensive armament was considered superfluous.

The Canberra B 2 was immediately put into production and was first delivered to the RAF in 1951, thereby beginning a service career which was to extend over a period of more than 30 years. Eventually the Canberra became one of the RAF's most versatile machines. The Royal Rhodesian Air Force acquired 15 B 2s in 1959, and these attractive bombers regularly visited South Africa. Canberras Nos 201 and 210 (RRAF) were the first of the type seen at Port Elizabeth while on a navigation exercise. With a smooth roar emanating from their turbojets they put on a good show over the Airport, performing impressive tight turns.

Fitted with two 6 500 lb (4 860 kg) thrust Rolls-Royce Avon engines, the B 2 carried a 6 000 lb (2 700 kg) bomb load and attained a maximum speed of 570 mph (917 km), a climb rate of 3 800 ft/min (1 158 m/min) and a range of 2 656 miles (4 274 km).

Notes on the finish
Canberras Nos 201 and 210 wore a Silver overall finish with matt Black anti-glare nose panels. Three silver-bladed assegais were superimposed on the red of their RAF D-type roundels. In the case of No 210 the serial number (RRAF 201) appeared in the usual rear fuselage position and was repeated on the nosewheel doors. No markings were worn on the undersides.

In 1966 Canberras Nos 208 and 212 (RRAF) were seen in (BS) gloss Dark Earth overall with a (BS) Dark Green disruptive pattern on the top surfaces only. The roundels on the fuselage and top surfaces, as well as the fin flashes, where the same size as the RAF D type, but were actually of a C type although with a slightly narrower White ring and painted in BS Aircraft Blue and BS Post Office Red. A single assegai was painted on the centre-line, with a Silver blade and Light Stone shaft. The serial numbers appeared in the same positions in the Silver scheme. All gloss colours were later changed to matt finishes.

Flying over Port Elizabeth in 1966, the early-morning sun is reflected off the cigar-shaped fuselage and broad-cord wings of this English Electric Canberra of the Royal Rhodesian Air Force.

Breguet Alizé

The French aircraft carrier *Foch* passed Algoa Bay in April 1966 on her way to the Pacific, where nuclear tests were scheduled to take place. Two of her aircraft were flown off to pick up mail at Port Elizabeth, and Breguet Alizés Nos 11 and 27 of Flotille 9F arrived over the Port Elizabeth Airport at midday.

When they took off about two hours later, their Rolls-Royce Dart turboprops sounded like the humming buzz of bees.

Although the Alizé entered service with the French Navy in 1959, Flotilles 4F and 6F are still operating the type – recently modernized to extend their service life. The Indian Navy, which took delivery of twelve examples in 1961, operated them with success against submarines during the short war with Pakistan in 1971.

The Alizé (trade wind) is a fascinating machine, which shows off its size when seen on the ground. A successful anti-submarine aircraft requires space for radar and electronic equipment, a weapons bay, adequate fuel storage and a crew of at least three, and the Alizé has achieved all this in a remarkably compact package. Two shapely wing-mounted fairings were installed to accommodate the undercarriage with its small-diameter twin wheels. With a retractable dustbin radar scanner, it looked like a mini-Shackleton.

Fitted with a single 1 975 shp (1 476 kW) Rolls-Royce Dart Da 7 turboprop engine, a mission speed of 285 mph (459 km/h), a climb rate of 1 380 ft/min (421 m/min), a ceiling of 20 000 ft (6 096 m) and an endurance of 4½ hours are attained. The weapons bay accommodates a heavy torpedo or depth charges and two Nord AS 12 missiles or six 5-inch air-to-surface rockets under the wings.

Notes on the finish

Until 1987 Alizés had one operational scheme. The top surfaces of wings, tailplane, fuselage decking and vertical tail were Extra Dark Sea Grey. All undersides were in a Sky colour very slightly darker than BS Sky. On Nos 11 and 27 the colours, which were originally semi-gloss, had become weathered. The roundels were the standard Aéronavale type and the aircraft number was painted on the fuselage aft of the roundel in Black and repeated in White on the upper starboard wing while a roundel was worn on the port wing, in accordance with Nato practice. This was repeated on the undersides, except that the numerals were Black. The number was painted in miniature on the nose under the gloss Black spinner as well as on the sides above the nosewheel door. The radome was Brown, the de-icing boots on the wing leading edges matt Black, and the wingtips and fairing behind the canopy Yellow. The 9F badge was placed ahead of the cockpit entry.

The recently-modernized aircraft have adopted a new scheme of White in place of Sky, and Pale Blue-Grey upper surfaces – very much like the early RAF Shackletons. The positions of the numbers remain as before, except that the word Marine is painted in Black forward of the fuselage roundel.

An English Electric Canberra 'on the deck' over the Karoo not far from Graaff-Reinet in 1967.

English Electric Canberra B(I) 12

In 1962 the SAAF ordered six Canberra B(I) 8s for high-altitude reconnaissance and tactical bombing missions and three T 4s for conversion training. The SAAF aircraft, as well as twelve built for New Zealand, were redesignated B(I) 12. In May 1967 five of the reformed 12 Squadron's B(I) 12s visited Port Elizabeth, and of these Nos 452 and 453 were fitted with gun packs. These very popular aeroplanes have rendered exceptional service and continue to fly on operations, mainly in the high-altitude reconnaisance role.

A major difference compared to previous Canberras was an asymetrically positioned fighter-type cockpit canopy and a bomb bay redesigned to accommodate a removable gun pack housing four 20-mm cannon. Such an installation was used on some B 6s intended for intruder operations prior to the introduction of the B(I) 8.

Although built by English Electric and Blackburn (two companies which hadn't established a long association with South Africa like Avro, de Havilland and Hawker), the Canberra and Buccaneer nevertheless continued the tradition of a strong British influence on this country's aviation history. Sadly though, these two exceptionally successful and popular types were the last, for political issues have swept away traditions.

Notes on the finish
Originally the B(I) 12s were finished in Satin Silver overall and wore standard Castle insignia and fin flashes. Large Black fuselage serial numbers were displayed and were worn in the standard size according to RAF practice on the undersides. The 12 Squadron badge was painted on the fin.

The Silver T 4s were finished with Day-Glo wing and fuselage bands as well as a Light Earth fin panel, while matt Black was used for the anti-glare panel on the nose. Currently both the B 12 and T 4 Canberras serving with the SAAF are finished in matt Photo Reconnaissance Unit Blue overall, without insignia and with only the serial number painted in small numerals on the rear of the fuselage.

A Sud-Est Alouette III circles the Greek cargo ship Evdokia, *in danger of sinking in June 1979, while a second helicopter lifts a crewman to safety.*

Right: *The emblem of 16 Squadron.*

Sud-Est 3160 Alouette III

On 25 June 1973 'A' Flight of 16 Squadron, equipped with Sud-Est 3160 Alouette III helicopters, was transferred to the Port Elizabeth Air Force Base, thus opening a new chapter in the history of flying in the Eastern Cape. For the first time a military aviation unit stationed in the city for the purpose of training at the same time proved itself to be an invaluable asset, able to serve the general welfare of the community whenever required.

A typical maritime rescue, for example, was that undertaken when the Greek cargo ship *Evdokia* began shipping water during a storm along the East Cape coast. Under extremely adverse conditions two 16 Squadron Alouettes rescued most of the crew (seven members stayed on as a skeleton crew) from the sinking ship. Comdt R. Penhall, later Officer Commanding 16 Squadron in Port Elizabeth, then with the rank of captain, flew No 611 during this rescue. His flight engineer was the late WO Tommy Thomas.

With that peculiar (and now all too familiar) ringing whine of their turbines and the clap of their rotors the Alouettes (always with a standby crew ready) have saved lives from sinking ships, participated in air-sea rescue operations in co-operation with the National Sea Rescue Institute and come to the aid of people trapped in inaccessable spots during serious floods.

The story of rotorcraft in the service of the SAAF begins in 1957 when 17 Squadron, then equipped with Lockheed Venturas, reformed as the SAAF's first helicopter unit with three Sikorsky S-55s and one S-51. Eight SE3130 Alouette IIs were ordered by the SAAF in 1960 to increase their helicopter strength. These early turbine-powered helicopters proved such a success that the larger seven-seater Alouette III was ordered. More than 70 of these were ultimately acquired.

17 Squadron was made up of three flights, with 'A' flight at Pretoria, 'B' flight at Bloemfontein and 'C' flight at Cape Town. During 1968, when more Alouette IIIs were available, 'C' flight became the newly reformed 16 Squadron, later stationed at Durban. In July 1972 the unit (comprising 'A' and 'B' Flights) transferred to Bloemfontein, and in 1973 'A' Flight was established at the Port Elizabeth Air Force Base.

Developed from the Alouette II, the III was designed with a more powerful turboshaft engine and strengthened transmission and an enlarged cabin to accommodate a pilot and six passengers. Powered by a Turboméca Artouste IIIb engine of 570 shp (426 kW), a maximum speed of 130 mph (209 km/h), a range of 335 miles (539 km) and take-off weight of 5 000 lb (2 250 kg) were attained.

Notes on the finish
When delivered, the Alouettes wore the standard finish of matt BS Olive Drab overall with fuselage Castle insignia on the rotor centre line and a Yellow aircraft number centered on the elephant's ear filter. A number of machines, also in Olive Drab, wore a Gold police badge in place of the Castle insignia, or on the boom. The wording SA Police and SA Polisie appeared in Yellow below the badge on the fuselage or aft of the badge if on the boom. The rotors were painted matt Olive Drab.

On all helicopters a revised scheme of Matt Dark Earth with a disruptive pattern of Olive Drab is now standard. Two of the Port Elizabeth rescue machines have Day-Glo panels from the rear of the cockpit to the boom link, as well as on a two-metre long section of the upper surface. The rotors are finished in matt Dark Earth with Day-Glo tips and stripes on the tail unit.

Piaggio P-166S Albatross

When the Lockheed Ventura was retired in 1960, Douglas Dakotas serving with 27 Squadron (reformed in 1962) continued with close inshore maritime patrols in support of 35 Squadron's Shackletons until the SAAF replaced them with more suitable aircraft. The Piaggio P-166S was selected as the best suited for the task.

The Albatross, as it is referred to by the SAAF, entered service with 27 Squadron in 1969 and has, up to the present, rendered remarkably good service. Like the Venturas and Dakotas before them, they are regular callers at Port Elizabeth, usually stopping overnight. When taking off, or on approach, the assertive whining, rumbling crackle of their engines, due to the propeller pitch, sometimes sound like a ship's siren.

Developed from the attractive P-136 five-seater executive amphibian intended for the United States market, the P-166 (although land-based) maintains its flying boat configuration, with attractive high-mounted gull wings and pusher propellers. Piaggio designated the SAAF version (P-166S) with a longer nose to house the radar, and slender wing-tip tanks for increased range. The spacious cabin affords a good view and is ideal for low-level shipping reconnaisance and photography duties. Two 340 hp (254 kW) Lycoming GSO 480-BIC6 horizontally opposed engines with three-bladed pusher propellers make possible a speed of 222 mph (357 km/h) and a range of 1 200 miles (1 931 km).

Notes on the finish
The Albatross is finished with Dark Sea Grey wing and tailplane upper surfaces, including the engine nacelles and tops of the tanks, and gloss Photo Reconnaissance Unit Blue undersides. The fuselage decking and vertical tail surfaces are gloss White, separated by a thin BS Aircraft Blue stripe. The inner sides of the wingtip tanks, and the anti-glare panel, are matt Black, while the nose radome is semi-matt Black. The fuselage serial numbers (as originally worn) have been removed, and the last two numerals are repeated in Black on the top of the fin. As usual the full serial number is worn on the undersides. Red fuselage and wing propeller warning stripes are prominent, as are the Day-Glo long-range tank finlets. The 27 Squadron badge is positioned on the nose aft of the radome.

A Piaggio Albatross circles the SAS Maria van Riebeeck during exercises off the Eastern Cape coast in 1974. The Daphne-class submarine – lit by flares – ploughs through a heavy swell at dawn.

Aérospatiale SA321L Super Frelon

Developed from the SA3200 Frelon (Hornet), the Super Frelon was designed to meet an Aéronavale requirement, and therefore had a water-tight hull reminiscent of a flying boat, for landings at sea. When the SAAF ordered 16 Super Frelons (the largest helicopters built in Europe), they chose the non-amphibious version to meet their heavy-lift requirements.

Arriving in 1967, the first machines equipped the reformed 15 Squadron, which received all its aircraft by 1969. With the powerful throb of their rotors and three turbines, these reliable helicopters have always

been on hand and have given sterling assistance during national disasters, quite apart from their military operations. In the Eastern Cape, for example, they gave assistance during floods in 1968, and again in 1971, when the Gamtoos River Valley near Port Elizabeth was extensively flooded, cutting off many families from essential supplies. Super Frelon No 307 carried out a number of rescue operations and transported a great deal of emergency supplies.

The type's three Turboméca Turmo IIIC-6 turbo-shaft engines develop 1 320 shp (1 000 kW) each. With a payload of 8 818 lb (3 968

kg), a speed of 120 mph (193 km/h) and a range of 509 miles (819 km) is attained.

Notes on the finish

When originally delivered, the SAAF Super Frelons were finished in matt BS Olive Drab overall. Castle insignia were applied behind the window line, and all markings, including the serial number on the tail boom and nose, where in White. A finish of overall Matt Dark Earth and Olive Drab was adopted at a later stage. The serial numbers and insignia were replaced by a smaller Castle insignia on the fuselage spine. The main rotors were painted Dark Earth and the tail propeller matt Black, with Red-and-White tips. The cockpit interior is matt Black.

An Aérospatiale Super Frelon climbing out of the flooded Gamtoos River Valley in 1971 while assisting stranded farmers.

Aérospatiale SA330 Puma

Aérospatiale designed the SA330 as a tactical and logistics transport helicopter capable of all-weather operations. The first production aircraft flew in September 1968 in accordance with an Anglo-French agreement that the air arms of both these countries would purchase machines. The SAAF also ordered an initial batch of Pumas, as the type met their requirements for a medium-sized helicopter. Although they were third on the list, deliveries began in December 1969, suprisingly some time before the RAF received theirs.

The reformed 19 Squadron, equipped with the new Pumas, comprised two flights, one based at Swartkop and the other at Durban. With the rumble of their turbines, the clapping throb of their rotors and their speedy appearance, accentuated by their neatly retracted undercarriage, they are regularly seen over the Republic. Apart from their successes in the operational area they have also gone to sea aboard the fleet replenishment ship SAS *Tafelberg*. Apart from the examples serving with 19 Squadron, a few currently also serve with

30, 31 and 16 Squadrons – the latter unit based in Port Elizabeth.

Powered by two 1 575 shp (1 180 kW) Turboméca Turmo IVC turbines, a maximum speed of 182 mph (293 km/h) and a range of 355 miles (571 km) is attained. The Puma is capable of transporting 16 troops.

Notes on the finish
Pumas were originally finished in an overall Matt Olive Drab scheme with White serial numbers and standard Castle insignia, but this was later changed to the current scheme of Matt Dark Earth and Olive Drab with Dark Earth rotors.

Lockheed P-3 Orion

In February 1973 a very special aircraft arrived in Port Elizabeth. This was a Lockheed P-3 Orion of VXN-8, the US Navy's oceanographic development squadron, which oper-ated three Orions, two RP-3As ('Arctic Fox' and 'El Coyote') for studying polar ice fields and for underwater sounding of ocean depths and an RP-3D ('Roadrunner'), which called at Port Elizabeth as part of Project Magnet to chart the magnetic force fields of our planet.

The aircraft was equipped with complex survey instruments such as a neutron moni-tor, vector airborne magnetometer, radiation thermometer, laser altimeter and a cosmic ray avionics package, and for precise navigation it had a dual inertial navigation system like that used aboard Saturn V moon rockets, with its own onboard satellite tracking sys-tem. With a 17-man crew and a 1 200-gallon fuel tank installed in the weapons bay, it could undertake long-endurance tasks. Af-ter taking off from Port Elizabeth, for exam-ple, 'Roadrunner' flew directly to Perth, Australia.

Traditionally the builder of anti-submarine patrol aircraft for the US Navy (and subse-quently most for the western world as well), Lockheed designed the P-3 Orion as a re-placement for the P-2 Neptune. Like the Hudson and Ventura, the Orion was an adap-tion of a civil airliner. Using the Lockheed Electra's flying surfaces and power plant, much of the fuselage structure was retained and adapted to accommodate a variety of electronic equipment and combat stores re-quired for maritime operations. On 13 Au-gust 1961 the first Orions were delivered to patrol Squadrons UP-8 and UP-44.

Operating with numerous air arms, the Orion has established an enviable record. Where it not for political reasons, the SAAF's 35 Squadron would very likely be operating P-3Cs instead of Douglas Dakotas as replace-ments for its Avro Shackletons.

Powered by four 4 910 shp (3 132 kW) Alli-son T-56-A-14 turboprops, the Orion P-3B at-tains a maximum speed of 476 mph (766 km/h), a climb rate of 3 270 ft/min (1 000 m/min) and an operational radius of 2 000 miles (3 200 km) with three hours on station.

Notes on the finish

The Orion was finished in an overall gloss White scheme with a 'Red' rudder, lower fuselage trim, elevators and wing trailing edge. According to United States require-ments International Orange (FS 12197) was supposed to have been used, but the colour appeared darker and with a slight brown cast. Tests have shown that FS 12197 becomes darker due to weathering. All lettering was Black, while the spinners and propellers were painted matt Black and Grey, with Red-and-White tips.

A Transall C-160Z starting its let-down near Port Elizabeth in 1975. They are regularly seen over Algoa Bay, but now in their drab camouflage finish.

Transall C-160Z

The Transall C-160 was originally conceived to meet German and French requirements for a tactical cargo and troop transport to replace their Nord 2501 Noratlases. With a basic configuration resembling the Lockheed C-130 Hercules, including a rear loading ramp (which was found necessary as early as the 1940s when the Junkers Ju 352 Herkules was designed), the C-160 can carry bulky cargo or 80 paratroops.

When the SAAF were denied further Hercules, they ordered nine Transalls. Delivered during 1969-70 as equipment for 28 Squadron, they operate alongside the Hercules. With two engines in place of the Hercules' four, a slightly lower load capacity and performance are attained, but both machines have an exceptional record in spite of operating in rough conditions. Accompanied by the deep, mellow tone of their turboprops, the Transalls are regularly seen throughout the Republic.

Their two Rolls-Royce Tyne engines (the most powerful turboprops in general service in the West) develop 6 100 shp (4 600 kW) each, allowing a maximum speed of 333 mph (536 km/h) and a range of 2 832 miles (4 558 km) with a payload of 17 640 lb (7 938 kg) and an all-up weight of 112 435 lb (50 596 kg).

Notes on the finish
The Transalls were originally finished in natural metal with gloss White fuselage decking and an Insignia Blue separating line which bordered the Castle insignia, as on the Hercules. The words SA Air Force/SA Lugmag were painted in the same Blue within the white decking behind the cockpit. The serial number was painted in Black on the natural metal behind the cockpit and was repeated on the fin above the flash. The de-icing boots and nose radome were in semi-matt Black and the anti-glare panel in matt Black. The 28 Squadron badge was positioned below the rear cockpit window.

close rivals to the Supermarine machines in Schneider Trophy competitions. During the war their fighters (the C200, C202 and C205) were among the best Italy produced. When powered by the Daimler-Benz 605 engine, for example, the C205 was an extremely potent combat aircraft.

In the 1960s Aermacchi agreed to allow South Africa to licence-build the MB326, and as a result competition from Britain and France was eliminated. Known as the Impala 1, it became the first aeroplane produced by the new Atlas Aircraft Corporation. Initially complete aircraft were sent from Italy for assembly, but as production progressed, so did the local content, until almost entire aircraft were built by Atlas.

Proving well suited to its task, the SAAF inevitably sought to adapt the airframe for close-support and counter-insurgency operations. Aermacchi therefore developed the MB326KC – a single-seat version with wing hardpoints and two Defa 30-mm cannon. Designated the Impala 2, this aircraft (also built by Atlas) has seen considerable service in the Operational Area.

With a 3 410 lb (1 550 kg) thrust Bristol/ Rolls-Royce Viper 540 turbojet, a maximum speed of 506 mph (814 km/h), a climb rate of 4 420 ft/min (1 347 m/min), a range of 1 035 miles (1 666 km) and a ceiling of 41 000 ft (12 497 m) are attained.

Notes on the finish
The Impala 1s are finished in Silver overall with a matt Black anti-glare panel, inner surfaces of wingtip tanks and wing fences.

An Aermacchi Impala 1 of 6 Squadron heads for Pretoria. The Sundays River mouth and the curve of Algoa Bay can be clearly seen against a background of early-morning sun, cloud and wisps of mist drifting from the land mass.

Aermacchi MB-326M Impala 1

When Impala 1s replaced the Harvards of 6 'City of Port Elizabeth' Squadron in 1975, the type was already established as the standard SAAF advanced trainer. Designed and built in Italy as the Aermacchi MB-326M, the Impala was evolved by a firm which had established a tradition of designing high-performance aircraft. Before World War II Macchi built high-speed seaplane racers that became well known as world speed record-holders, and

The emblem of 6 Squadron.

Hawker Hunter FGA 9

Although South Africa never operated the Hawker Hunter (one of Britain's most successful and attractive fighters), it is fitting that they were seen in our skies, if only to symbolically continue the link with Hawkers. In 1963 the Royal Rhodesian Air Force re-equipped their 1 Squadron with twelve Hunter FGA 9s. Clearly a development of the Sea Hawk by way of the P1081 Hunter, the first successful British swept-wing fighter to join the RAF, set a new standard in armament. With four 30-mm Aden cannon (with the same development connection as the Defa), it was a highly successful trans-sonic day fighter.

As development progressed, the Hunter became a versatile aircraft with versions which included the FGA 9, the FR 10 and the GA 11 for the Royal Navy. A delightful aeroplane to handle, it served with numerous air arms. Powered by a 10 000 lb (4 536 kg) thrust Rolls-Royce Avon 203 or 207 engine, a maximum speed of 715 mph (1 150 km/h), a climb rate of 17 500 ft/min (5 334 m/min), a ceiling of 55 000 ft (16 764 m) and a range of 1 840 miles (2 961 km) were attained.

Notes on the finish
Hunter R1280 (seen over the Transvaal in July 1974) was finished in overall gloss Dark Earth with Dark Green in a disruptive pattern on the top surfaces. The new Green, White and Gold insignia was painted on the nose and there were matching fin flashes, but no wing roundels. The serial number was painted on the small nosewheel door but did not appear on the rear fuselage.

Showing off its sleek, sharklike lines, a Rhodesian Air Force Hawker Hunter performs a shallow dive over the Transvaal landscape in 1974.

Dassault Mirage F1

With its undercarriage detracted, the beautiful, clean shape of the Dassault Mirage F1 takes on the appearance of a giant predatory insect.

Designed as a replacement for the delta-winged Mirage III, the Mirage F1 reverted to the swept-wing concept. Automatic leading edge flaps fitted to the razor-thin mainplane considerably improved combat manoeuvrability, especially at slower speeds. The F1CZ version delivered to the SAAF in 1975 equipped 3 Squadron. A Cyrano IV radar system enabled the CZ to operate as an all-weather interceptor, while the F1AZs of 1 Squadron (also delivered in 1975) were equipped with a smaller ranging system and therefore operated as a clear-weather interceptor or in the ground-attack role.

Powered by a 15 873 lb (7 143 kg) thrust SNECMA-Atar 9 K-50 engine, a maximum speed of Mach 2.2 and a considerably improved range over its predecessors was attained. These attractive fighters with their sharp nose, beautifully contoured fuselage and shoulder wing are still very active.

Notes on the finish

When delivered, the finish of the Mirage F1s was the standard SAAF Olive Drab, Deep Buff and Light Admirality Grey. The F1s were the first aircraft to wear the new low visibility scheme comprising three colours: Grey Blue, Dark Grey and Pale Lavender Grey.

General comments on aircraft finishes

Like a sculptor, who has to gain a detailed knowledge of the human skeletal structure before he can create his model's outer form and texture, the dedicated aviation artist must be completely knowledgeable about his field of interest. Apart from the fluid, magnificent background of airspace, it is essential to undertake a long-term study of the exciting world of aero-engineering, and its unequalled rate of development from timber and fabric, through stressed alloy skinning and pressings to the computerized milling of metals and the use of plastics, to achieve the varying shapes and structures dictated by the frontiers of aerodynamic evolution. Possibly the most important single factor for the artist is the fascinating and often frustrating subject of aircraft finishes and markings: no matter how accurate the airframe representation, the whole work loses its integrity if what amounts to a thin coating of colour is incorrectly portrayed.

Although South Africa was off the main stream of aviation activity, it has hosted most of the world's famous aircraft, including many that served with the SAAF, especially during World War II. Throughout those years machines delivered from Britain or the United States wore the colour schemes of their respective air arms and were repainted, sometimes partially, to adapt to local conditions. This has created a rich variety of finishes, and these have become a unique field of research which can ultimately be of great assistance to those involved in museum and private projects to restore aircraft that served in South Africa.

Many of these non-standard colours or variations of standard colours are discussed, with reference to samples removed from actual aircraft, and are in turn related to the individual colour details contained in the descriptions accompanying each painting. These 'master colours', standard or otherwise, have been identified with reference to the following internationally recognized documents: British Air Ministry Standard Colours, 1942; British Standard (BS) 381c, 1964 and 1980; US Federal Standard (FS) 595; *Methuen Handbook of Colour*; and *The Official Monogram Painting Guide to Luftwaffe Aircraft, 1935-1945*.

It must be carefully borne in mind that the 'master' colour reference which identifies the actual colour applied to the airframe, according to official BSC, FS standards or whatever, is merely the starting point. In the creation of a painting numerous variations of the 'master' are used to compensate for variations in scale, light and shade conditions and weathering. As a simple example, the depiction on p 98 of the 60 Squadron Mosquito illustrates the procedure. Delivered as a comparatively new photo-reconnaisance machine, it was finished in the prescribed overall matt Photo Reconnaissance Unit Blue specified in the 1942 AM colour standards. Identical to

the current BS 381c, PRU Blue 636 is therefore the 'master'. However, when 60 Squadron flew their Mosquitoes to South Africa, they had served on operations for two years. Taken together with the fact that they had been painted with a matt finish, they had developed a washed-out tone on their upper surfaces. PRU Blue contains a Yellow constituent more influenced by ultra-violet light than its Black, White and Ultramarine components, so its hue had also slightly changed to one that appeared more blue on the washed-out areas. Add to this the contrast of bright sunlight and deep shadow on the airframe, and it will be seen that nowhere in the painting is the 'master' actually applied, only its variations, which give the illusion of weathered PRU Blue.

The first aircraft operated by the SAAF – those of the Imperial Gift – retained their original finishes. This finish was described as khaki-brown by the late Pat (Syd) Neave (a friend of Major Allister Miller and most of the Union Airways' aircrews, a pilot himself, a scale modeller and someone who recorded aviation events such as the 1925 SAAF Air Mail Service).

According to various records the three pigments adopted for RFC aircraft were Yellow Ochre, Black and Oxide Red. Coincidentally, these same three colours are found on rock painting rendered in Spain 20 000 years ago which represent some of the first art recorded. PC 10 (Pigmented Cellulose or Protective Coating 10) was said to have comprised Yellow Ochre and Black, whereas PC 12 contained Oxide Red as an additional protection against ultra-violet light for machines operating overseas. However, not having had the opportunity to examine machines with these finishes, apart from the DH 6 remains at the SAAF Museum, I cannot authoritively discuss them, although I did carry out certain tests which proved interesting.

Taking samples of the three generally recognized variations of Yellow Ochre (Methuen 5C7, 5C6 and 5D5), I added Black to each, thus forming a sequential strip mix starting with the ochre and ending with black. Although a minor difference between the ochres was noticed, when black was added they changed to light khaki, darker khaki with a green cast, still darker khaki with a predominantly green cast, dark green (identical to the current BS 381c Dark Green), black green, and black, but with no suggestion of brown. The DH 9 (F1258) in the Musée de l'Air, Paris, has a green finish which conforms to this mix. On the other hand, when Oxide Red was added to the mixture, a brown cast developed, like that on the remains of the DH 6 at the SAAF Museum. In fact, depending on the amount of Red and Black added, a hue identical to Dark Earth evolved. Mixing black and red on their own created a deep, hard, almost purple brown that I have never recorded on an aircraft. The

khaki-brown on the SAAF's DH 6s and DH 9s was more like Dark Earth, but whether it was PC 10 or PC 12, I cannot be sure.

All forms of camouflage disappeared when overall Silver became standard as the most practical finish for military aircraft during the years immediately following World War I. The RAF A-type roundel adopted by the SAAF in place of the original four-colour insignia had an Orange centre. The blue, very much like AM matt Blue, had a strong Ultramarine cast.

During the late 1930s, when war seemed inevitable, the RAF once more introduced a camouflage scheme comprising Dark Green and Dark Earth which was applied in a disruptive pattern and referred to as the Temperate Land scheme. These two successful colours, based on the Yellow Ochre, Black and Red Oxide mixtures of World War I, have remained in use with the SAAF to this day. The first camouflaged aircraft in South Africa were the initial batch of Hawker Hurricanes, a Fairey Battle and a Bristol Blenheim which were accepted for evaluation, while the Avro Anson GR Is employed on coastal patrol duties were the first aircraft in regular service with a camouflage scheme. They were delivered with standard RAF Dark Green and Dark Earth upper surfaces and Sky (type 'S') undersides, but this pale green grey was considered unsuitable for the strong blue of the South African skies, so Sky Blue was introduced as the standard underside finish for SAAF aircraft. Basically four different underside blues, of which I have samples, were used in SAAF service, and there were also a few odd colours, which are discussed.

Most of the coastal Ansons were painted with a blue for which I have found no official title, and it is referred to in this work as SAAF Sky Blue 'A'. Virtually identical to FS 35190, or a variation of FS 35189, and evidently an overcoat in each case, these comparatively dark colours had a high production standard, for my three samples (two from Ansons and one from a Hawker Hartbees) are identical. SAAF Sky Blue 'B', used on many Hawker Hurricanes and Lockheed B-34 Venturas, is a pale version of AM Azure – very much like Methuen 21B4 (FS 35450 with a violet cast). Characteristically the influence of ultra-violet light was severe, changing the hue to a pale powder blue. AM Azure and FS 35231 Azure were also in regular use, mainly on machines flown down from the Middle East. These colours varied, for the FS Azure was distinctly darker than the AM colour. A number of Venturas and Curtiss P-40N Kittyhawks were finished in the FS paint.

A few additional underside blues need mentioning. The AM Light Mediterranean Blue is a colour seldom referred to, but was used on many SAAF aircraft operating in North Africa. It was recorded on the undersides of two Hurricanes of 11 Operational Training Unit newly painted in Dark Earth and Middle Stone – both without the usual Yellow bands. Although I cannot substantiate the fact, some of 60 Squadron's Mosquitoes could have been finished in Light Mediterranean Blue if they had been repainted in Italy. At least one 11 OTU Hurricane had AM Sky Blue undersides, while another (rather dirty) aircraft had a paler, slightly more grey version of SAAF Sky Blue 'A' over a dark version of Azure, possibly as a substitute for Light Mediterranean Blue (see p 80).

As for the upper surface colours, they also varied when aircraft were repainted. Pieces of Dark Green and Dark Earth fabric in my collection had not been affected by ultra-violet light because they were removed from behind the wing fillet of an Airspeed Oxford built in 1942. The Dark Earth is identical to the current BS 450, but the Dark Green is slightly lighter than BS 641. As the war progressed, variations of these two colours were recorded, possibly due to poor production colour standards, intermixing, or the use of Australian dopes. A Hurricane was painted with a variation of Dark Green which resembled Australian Forest Green (FS 34058/FS 34077) and Earth Brown (FS 30099). Another painted with Dark Earth had large areas of a brown which was very near to FS 30062 in place of Dark Green. Light Green and Light Earth were applied to a few Ansons, possibly by mistake or as a convenience when repairs were carried out. Both colours were, however, painted as anti-glare panels on the noses and nacelles of most Anson trainers when Silver upper surfaces were introduced.

Aircraft delivered from the United States in the FS equivalents of Dark Green and Dark Earth showed a subtle difference which was discernible when they were parked alongside machines painted in AM finishes. Instead of adopting Dark Green, these aircraft were painted in Olive Drab (FS 34087 – dark hue), which had a slight yellow cast and was a fraction paler than Dark Green, while the FS 30118 Dark Earth was slightly more olive and darker than the AM colour. The overall effect was that the two colours contrasted less, as is illustrated on p 87. During World War II the FS 34087 Olive Drab was used in two shades. One, with a brown cast, appears in the current FS Standard, while the other (the dark shade used with Dark Earth or as a US colour – see p 73) was close to the current FS 34086. Wartime colour photographs of US Douglas C-47 Dakotas clearly illustrate that both versions were used during the war. Neither must be confused with the current BS 298 Olive Drab used with Dark Earth on SAAF aircraft.

As Port Elizabeth was a training station during World War II, many aircraft with Yellow as a dominant finish operated from there. AM Yellow, FS 33538 and a South African version nearly as light as FS 33655 were in regular use, and of all colours this became the most susceptible to adulteration. While the original colours were more than likely according to official standards, their brightness and the capability of cellulose to dissolve old paint resulted in some aircraft with dirty tinted undersides quite apart from the usual splattering of oil and dirt. A sample in my collection (Methuen 4 B8/C8) identified on a number of Ansons during 1945, where the colour appeared in patches, and in a few cases on the entire underside of an aircraft, appeared to be a batch to which a minor quantity of Black, Dark Green or Dark Earth had been added. The underside of the Anson portrayed on p 85 was

finished in Methuen 4 D8, which was more like Pale Olive than Yellow. Towards the end of the war many Ansons and Oxfords sported an original underside hue which had been liberally patched with some of the variations mentioned, and was also coated with dirt.

In 1942, when 25 Squadron's B-34 Venturas arrived in their RAF bomber scheme of Dark Green, Dark Earth and Sky (FS alternatives), SAAF Sky Blue 'B' was applied to most undersides. Two machines had 'White' undersides and flanks, with Dark Green and Dark Earth upper flying surfaces and fuselage decking. The underside colour was actually a broken white, very pale grey, much like FS 35630. It is portrayed on p 52, where the insignia White is illustrated as a pure colour in comparison to the fuselage colour.

The PV-1 Venturas that later replaced the B-34s displayed the new standard US Navy three-tone scheme which developed interesting characteristics after two or three years in the South African environment. The scheme comprised FS 37875 White undersides, FS 35164 Intermediate Blue flanks, FS 35042 Sea Blue fuselage decking, upper surfaces of motor nacelles and curved leading edges, and FS 25042 semi-gloss Sea Blue main and tailplane upper surfaces. The semi-gloss paint was more permanent than its matt equivalent, which rapidly developed a washed-out appearance, and therefore appeared even darker and cleaner when seen against the faded decking. The overall effect was as though four different colours had been used. Because of its porosity, the matt White undersides were impregnated by dirt and red highveld dust, so that it discoloured in areas (mainly on the fuselage) to a pale grey near to FS 37722, with splashes of FS 33617. Another rare Ventura scheme, seen on 17 Squadron's PV-1s from the Mediterranean Theatre, was determined by the fact that these coastal patrol bombers undertook night operations. As a result their undersides were painted Black (Night), while their US Navy Sea Blue and Intermediate Blue upper surfaces were retained instead of the prescribed AM Dark Sea Grey.

As the war progressed, Fleet Air Arm aircraft were regularly seen at South African coastal air stations. There were a few exceptions to the AM Temperate Sea scheme of Extra Dark Sea Grey and Dark Slate Grey in a disruptive pattern, with Sky undersides. US Navy aircraft such as the Vought Kingfisher were painted in FS 35189 Blue Gray and FS 36440 Light Gray (FS 36118 Sea Gray was also used for upper surfaces), while early examples of the Vought Corsair were painted in the Temperate Sea scheme, but using FS colours, as illustrated on p 78. Furthermore the AM colours were affected by ultra-violet light, as was the case with Grumman Hellcats prepared at Wingfield for service in the Pacific. New Extra Dark Sea Grey and Dark Slate Grey contrasted considerably less than Dark Green and Dark Earth, with the result that if they had faded, or were scratched and caked with dirt, they harmonized into one colour, which from a distance looked like an overall grey. The underside Sky also lost some of its initial cleanness to take on the appearance of

a pale dirty grey. The picture on p 77 gives a good impression of this condition.

Fleet Air Arm Bristol Beaufighter IIs operating in South Africa were also finished in the standard Temperate Sea scheme with AM Azure undersides according to the official requirement. Beaufighter W8R (see p 93), however, sported the very pale AM Sky Blue, while others were correctly finished in Azure.

Without a doubt AM Sky was a successful colour for the temperate European Theatre, but seemed very yellow-green in an African or Pacific environment, where the sky usually is a strong blue with a purple-grey cast. In addition the tonal weakness of the Yellow constituent was easily broken down by ultra-violet light, whereas the other pigments (Ultramarine, Black and White) remained more intact, in the form of pale dirty grey with a hint of Sky. Unaffected Sky, removed from a Fairey Swordfish (HS256), matches the current BS 210, wartime AM Sky and FS Sky. Seen together with a piece of underside skinning from a Kittyhawk (No 5106) which was also finished in FS Sky (a rarity among SAAF Kittyhawks), both conform to official standards, thus proving that the original colours were of a high production standard.

In 1948, when the Hawker Sea Furies and Fireflies of HMS Vengeance (15th Carrier Air Group) visited South Africa, they were painted in the AM Temperate Sea scheme with an immaculate high gloss finish. Their Sky undersides were a true representation of the official colour, with no fading or discolouration, and were nothing like the washed-out hues seen during the war. The paintings on pp 93 and 112 clearly illustrate the variations between matt and gloss FAA finishes.

In August 1972 I initiated a series of simple tests using BSC 1964 cellulose aircraft series fitted to a plate that had been secured to an out-building roof. The following was observed during monthly checks over a period of two years: After two months, matt Sky was the first colour to change, and six months later it was very slightly more grey than the gloss sample, which had remained unaltered. After sixteen months matt Sky had become a more blue-grey than the gloss because the Yellow had evidently faded out of the surface layer, having been broken down by ultra-violet light. By this time the other matt colours had also become washed-out. The most altered after Sky was PRU Blue, which had faded to an even blue, losing some of its yellow cast, while matt RAF Blue-Grey (FS Sea Blue) had faded to a grey. The gloss colours started losing their shine after between nine and twelve months and after two years had also begun fading rapidly. Two colours (108 Aircraft Blue and 592 International Orange) retained most of their gloss and colour, but the orange took on a slight brown cast.

During the early post-war years the SAAF surprisingly adopted Sky as the standard underside finish for Venturas and the few Hurricanes remaining in service, until the arrival of Supermarine Spitfires in 1947 (pp 108 and 109). Well-maintained semi-gloss paintwork kept the standard colours from deteriorating, although when replaced by PRU Blue in 1959, two additional variations of Sky were recorded (pp 126 and 127). The first Spitfire IXs to serve with 1 Squadron were attractively painted in the same scheme as the Hurricanes, which scheme included C-type roundels. However, most Spitfires were repainted in a Dark Green, Ocean Grey and Medium Sea Grey semi-gloss finish without Sky spinners and fuselage bands. Samples from these aircraft in my collection reveal that most of the Dark Green was identical to BS 641, but a lighter variation like that used during World War II was also used. The SAAF Medium Sea Grey is slightly darker than BS 637, and the Ocean Grey is also very slightly darker than the AM standard, while a sample of the original RAF paint is actually slightly lighter than the standard, of which I have a sample.

Towards the end of the war most FAA aircraft obtained from the United States were painted in the new US Navy finish of gloss Sea Blue. For example the Hellcats of 881 Squadron at Wingfield sported this blue finish, but their South East Asia Command insignia were applied using SAAF Insignia Blue 'AA', which is somewhat lighter than Sea Blue.

Insignia colours varied according to official dictates (especially the blue), but during World War I changes were made according to the availability of pigments or variables in mixing. The first SAAF aircraft were delivered with RAF Ultramarine, White and Vermillion roundels, which were modified to a new South African design by replacing the White with Green and Gold, the latter adjoining the Ultramarine. The freshly painted Brunswick Green and Deep Ochre Yellow contrasted strongly with the original British colours. In the years immediately following World War I, when the RAF adopted modified Red and Blue (colours which are said to be the same as AM matt Red and Blue), the SAAF also used the same A-type roundels, excepting that Orange replaced the Red.

At the outbreak of World War II, former RAF aircraft serving in South Africa – mainly at the Air Schools – wore A, A1 and B roundels with Orange centres, and the original AM matt Blue. When the post-1942 C-type roundels with AM Blue (Dark Indigo) and Red (Dull Brick) were introduced, the latter colour was replaced by Light Orange on SAAF aircraft. There were variations of the blue which (in the case of A or B roundels) was mixed without the British Ultramarine base. Two common hues are re-

ferred to as SAAF Roundel Blue 'AA' which is close to FS 35102 but with a tendency towards FS 35109, and SAAF Roundel Blue 'BB' with a more grey cast which places it roughly between FS 35080 and FS 35164. SAAF Sky Blue 'A' was seen as an insignia colour on numerous overall Yellow Tiger Moths.

It must be remembered that the colours referred to are 'masters' which were changed in time by ultra-violet breakdown, especially in the case of local colours not containing Ultramarine. For example AM matt Blue generally stood up well, but AM (Dark) Blue lost its dark tone and washed out to a colour almost as light as FS 35109 on the upper surface roundels of II OTU Hurricanes. In some cases, on the other hand, when the SAAF repainted B, C and C1 roundels (mainly on Ansons and a few Hurricanes), 'AA' or 'BB' was used, at times with the retention of the RAF Red centres. These incongruous roundels are illustrated in the paintings on pp 82 and 85. The individual insignia descriptions accompanying each painting show that unlike RAF insignia, those of the SAAF varied to a great extent. The reason was that the arrival of so many machines from other theatres made it difficult to maintain a defined system.

In the years following World War II, however, it was a different matter, for D-type roundels were standardized, as they were in the RAF. BS (1964) 108 Aircraft Blue was adopted, together with 557 Light Orange, and a Springbok motif was introduced. Incidentally, the same Blue, together with BS 538 Post Office Red, replaced AM Blue and Red on RAF and FAA aircraft in 1948, as illustrated on p 112. In 1974 SABS 1091-1975 was introduced as a colour standard for South African use. Most of the BS aircraft colours are listed, but the names of a few were altered. For example Flag Blue (F04) matches Roundel Blue (BS (1980)), while Flag Orange (B20), currently used on SAAF insignia, does not have a BS equivalent but is somewhere between FS 12215 and FS 12473. A variation found on RAF aircraft is that BS (1964) 108 Aircraft Blue has been discontinued in favour of BS (1980) 110 Roundel Blue, which has less of an Ultramarine tone.

During the early post-war years Silver and natural metal again became international standard finishes, as was the case directly after World War I. More recently camouflage has been re-introduced, and the colours, which have generally been to official specifications, have been

constant. These can be seen to advantage in numerous books containing good colour photographs.

A wartime aircraft I examined in detail during 1955 cannot pass without comment. The Messerschmitt Me 262 B-1A/U-1 (see p 123) was painted to a finish not fully understood at the time, for the colours were not on any of the known German Reichsluftfahrtministerium (RLM) standards. However, it was later established that the Dornier Do 335 at the Smithsonian Institution (which was stored in the open) had faded light green and brown green paintwork very much like that on South Africa's Me 262. In addition the Do 335 painting guide, which was obtained later, specified new colours RLM 81 and 82, and I therefore designated the colours of the SAAF Me 262 as such, together with RLM 76. *The Official Monogram Painting Guide to Luftwaffe Aircraft, 1935-1945* is the best source for checking the 'master' colours. Samples removed from the South African Me 262 were checked against the hues on p 59 of this guide, with the following interesting conclusions:

RLM 81 – Brown-Violet. My sample of this colour is slightly darker and a fraction browner than that in the book, which may be due to production standards.

RLM 83 – Light Green. My sample has a slighty more yellow hue than that in the book.

RLM 76. The field colour on the fuselage, to which I refer as RLM 76, does not match the RLM 76 on p 59 of the book, but is identical to the right-hand sample on p 41, which is listed as a late-production alternative to RLM 76, with a slight green hue.

As a matter of interest, four samples from different aircraft in my collection are almost identical. The fascinating effect of the air-brushed application of the three colours on the South African Me 262 are described in the text on p 122. A detailed description of this aircraft's finish was published in the April 1975 issue of *Air International*, including full colour profiles.

It is hoped that these descriptions of particular colours and their peculiarities (based on personal examinations and samples from the actual aircraft), will be a guide to the devoted restorer, modeller or historian and help him to gain an insight into the 'unofficial' or adulterated versions of standard schemes portrayed in many of the paintings which recreate machines the like of which we will not see again.

National Aircraft Insignia

Great Britain

1 Royal Flying Corps/Royal Air Force roundel, 1915-1937. (Ultramarine and Vermillion.)

2 RFC/RAF rudder stripes, 1915-1937.

3 RAF A-type roundel, 1937-1942.*

4 RAF A1-type roundel, 1937-1942.*

5 RAF B-type roundel, 1937-1942.*

6 RAF 24 x 27 inch fin flash, 1937-1942.*

7 RAF C-type roundel, 1942-1948. AM Blue and Red were later used in gloss paint.

8 RAF C1-type roundel, 1942-1948.

9 RAF C-type fin flash, 1942-1948.

10 Hybrid C and C1-type roundel with South East Asia Command rectangles. Recorded only on Avro Lancaster 'Aries'.

11 Fleet Air Arm small SEAC roundel, 1944-1945. C and C1-type roundels were overpainted in grey or green and a roundel with a smaller diameter, in AM Blue and White, was superimposed.

12 FAA standard SEAC roundel in AM Blue and White, 1944-1945.

13 FAA large SEAC roundel, 1945-1946. This is a standard roundel with a white outer ring and rectangles outlined in blue.

14 FAA SEAC fin flash, 1944-1946.

15 RAF D-type roundel, 1948-present. BS 108 Aircraft Blue and BS 538 Post Office Red are used. BS 108 was replaced by BS 110 Roundel Blue in 1980.

16 RAF standard fin flash, 1948-present.

South Africa

17 Standard SAAF insignia, 1921-1929.

18 Standard SAAF rudder stripes, 1921-1929.

19 SAAF A-type roundel, 1937-1942.

20 SAAF A1-type roundel, 1937-1942.

21 SAAF B-type roundel, 1941-1944.**

22 Improvised SAAF roundel, with 'AA' Blue used in A, A1 and B-type roundels, 1940-1946.

23 Improvised SAAF roundel, with 'BB' blue used in A, A1, and B-type roundels, 1940-1946.

24 SAAF A-type roundel with Sky Blue 'A', as used on some Tiger Moths. A paler blue was also recorded.

25 SAAF standard full fin flash.

26 SAAF C-type roundel, 1943-1948.**

27 SAAF C1-type roundel, 1943-1948.**

28 Hybrid SAAF C-type roundel with SAAF 'AA' Blue and AM Red, 1943-1945. Similar C1 and B-type roundels were recorded.

29 SAAF D-type roundel, 1948-1950. The BS 538 has been replaced by BS 557 Light Orange.

30 SAAF D-type fin flash, 1948-1950.

31 Springbok roundel, 1950-1957. This is a D-type roundel with an Orange springbok.

32 Castle insignia, 1957-present. In 1975 BS 108 Aircraft Blue was replaced by SABS FO4 Flag Blue. The springbok is in Gold.

33 Castle insignia painted with French Insignia Blue, as recorded on early Dassault Mirage IIICZs.

34 Castle insignia painted with US Insignia Blue, as recorded on Lockheed Hercules when first delivered.

United States

35 US Star insignia with Red inner circle, 1919-1942.

36 US Navy rudder stripes, 1919-1941. In 1941 horizontal Red stripes came into use.

37 US Star insignia, 1942-1943. From 1943 Blue-outlined rectangles were added.

38 US Star insignia, 1947-present, with Red stripes added to the Blue rectangles. The Blue is FS 35044 and the Red FS 31136.

Netherlands

39 Dutch flag insignia worn by the Netherlands East Indies Air Force, 1942-1946.

Japan

40 Japanese hinomaru insignia, which was outlined in white or placed on a white rectangle.

France

41 French roundel as worn on their military aircraft since the inception of military aviation in France.

42 Standard French rudder stripes. Before WW II maritime aircraft wore a black anchor on the rudder.

43 French Armée de l'Air roundel as used after World War II. A Deep Yellow outer ring has been added to the earlier insignia.

44 French Aéronavale roundel as used after World War II. A black anchor has been added to the standard roundel.

45 A rare Aéronavale fin flash, resembling an RAF type, recorded on French Maritime Reconnaissance Avro Lancasters. Most naval aircraft wore rudder stripes with a superimposed anchor.

Germany

46 Early Luftwaffe balkenkreuz insignia, as found on South Africa's Fieseler Fi 156 Storch and Focke-Wulf Fw 190.

47 Early Lufwaffe white-outlined hakenkreuz without black centre, as worn on dark vertical surfaces.

48 Late Luftwaffe white-outlined balkenkreuz, as worn on dark backgrounds, found on South Africa's Messerschmitt Me 262.

Rhodesia

51 Royal Rhodesian Air Force insignia, 1954-1963. This is an RAF D-type roundel with three Silver and Black assegais.

52 RRAF fin flash, 1954-1963.

53 RRAF insignia, 1963-1970. This is an RAF C-type roundel (the proportions differ) with a single Silver, Buff and Black assegai.

54 RRAF fin flash, 1963-1970.

55 Rhodesian Air Force insignia, 1970-1980. This is a Light Brunswick Green roundel with a Gold and Black lion.

56 Rhodesian Air Force fin flash, 1970-1980.

49 Late Luftwaffe black-outlined balkenkreuz, as worn on light backgrounds.

50 Late Luftwaffe black stencilled hakenkreuz, as worn on light vertical surfaces.

Through the years aircraft operating from South Africa have worn a large variety of national insignia, and many of these are mentioned in the text. Most of them may be identified on the illustrated aircraft, but the representations on these pages are included to facilitate such identification.

When referring to these examples, the forward direction is to the left. Although the colours of the British B-type roundel relate to the C and C1 types, it was also used with the A and A1 type. Not illustrated is the SAAF C-type fin flash, which was like the RAF type, but with Orange in place of Red.

The colours are rendered 'as new'. Many, especially the AM Blue used in the B and C-type roundels, faded very badly on mainplane upper surfaces.

* In the case of the 1937-1942 insignia AM Blue (Indigo) and AM Red (Brick) were specified, but earlier stocks of AM matt Blue and matt Red were often used, as illustrated.

** These are standard RAF insignia with Orange in place of the Red.

Official Colour Documents

For the benefit of readers who require the precise master values of colours referred to in this work, the following documents are available.

BSI Publications: 'BSD 381C: 1980. Colours for Identification, Coding and Specific Purposes'. Obtainable from BSI Publications Manager, 101 Pentonville Road, London N1 9ND, United Kingdom. BS 381C: 1948 and 1964 are out of print, but should prove of great value if they could be obtained privately.

General Services Administration: 'Federal Standard No 595A, Colors'. Obtainable from General Services Administration, Specification Section, Room 6662 (3FBP-S-W), 7th and D Streets SW, Washington DC, 20407, United States.

Kornerup, A. and Wanscher, J. H.: *Methuen Handbook of Colour*, Eyre Methuen, London. Obtainable through local bookshops.

Merrick, K. A. and Hitchcock, T. H.: *The Official Monogram Painting Guide to Luftwaffe Aircraft, 1933-1945*. Obtainable from Monogram Aviation Publications, 625 Edgebrook Drive, Boylston, Massachusetts, 01505, United States.

South African Bureau of Standards: 'SABS 1091-1975'. Obtainable from SA Bureau of Standards, Private Bag X191, Pretoria, 0001. In this guide most of the colours which originated in the BS system retain their international titles. The names of a few have changed, however, and this can be confusing. For example Post Office Red has become A09 Flag Red, Sky has become D40 Light Grey-Green, and Photo Reconnaissance Unit Blue has become F12 Slate, which must not be confused with Light Slate and Dark Slate as used by the RAF.

Tanner, John (Ed): *British Aviation Colours of World War Two*, RAF Museum Series, Vol. 3. This is the official guide to the camouflage, colours and markings of RAF aircraft from 1939 to 1945, but is out of print. Second-hand copies could possibly be obtained from the RAF Museum, Hendon, London, NW4, United Kingdom.

Bibliography

Brown, David: *The Seafire*, Ian Allen, Weybridge, 1973.

Brown, J. P.: *Carrier Operations in World War II. Vol I: The Royal Navy*, Ian Allen, Weybridge, 1968.

Doll, Thomas E., Jackson, Berkley R. and Riley, William E.: *Navy Air Colors*, Vols I and II, Squadron/Signal Publications, Carrollton, Texas, 1983 and 1985.

Gunston, Bill: *World Encyclopedia of Aero Engines*, Patrick Stephens, Wellingborough, 1986.

Hoffschmidt, Edward J.: *German Aircraft Guns, WWI-WWII*, WE Inc, Old Greenwich, Conn., 1969.

Jackson, A. J.: *Avro Aircraft Since 1908*, Putnam, London, 1965.

—: *De Havilland Aircraft Since 1915*, Putnam, London, 1962.

Lukins, A. H. (Comp): *The Book of Miles Aircraft*, Harborough Publishing Co, Leicester, 1946.

—: *The Book of Westland Aircraft*, Harborough Publishing Co, Leicester, 1946.

Mason, Francis K.: *Hawker Aircraft Since 1920*, Putnam, London, 1961.

Potgieter, Herman and Steenkamp, Willem: *Aircraft of the South African Air Force*, C. Struik, Cape Town, 1980.

Sturtivant, Ray: *Fleet Air Arm at War*, Ian Allen, Weybridge, 1982.

—: *The Squadrons of the Fleet Air Arm*, Air Britain, Tunbridge, 1984.

Swanborough, Gordon and Bowers, Peter M.: *United States Military Aircraft Since 1909*, Putnam, London, 1963.

—: *United States Navy Aircraft Since 1911*, Putnam, London, 1968.

Tanner, John (Ed): *British Aircraft Colours of World War Two*, Arms & Armour Press, London, 1976.

Thetford, Owen: *Aircraft of the Royal Air Force, 1918-1957*, Putnam, London, 1957.

—: *British Naval Aircraft, 1912-1958*, Putnam, London, 1958.

Thorpe, Donald W.: *Japanese Naval Air Force Camouflage and Markings, World War II*, Aero Publishers, Fallbrook, 1977.